Discovering History

THE ROMAN EMPIRE

STEVE LANCASTER

Series Editors
**NEIL TONGE &
PETER HEPPLEWHITE**

To Lisa Fabry

Preface

The author wishes to acknowledge the help and advice of Lisa Fabry, Richard Holmes, Madelin Huws, Jane and Tony Lancaster, Nicholas On and Jeremy Paterson. Any mistakes are, of course, the author's responsibility.

Steve Lancaster
June, 1991

Note to teachers

1. **The Focus pages**
    Each chapter contains a Focus page which aims to engage the reader, excite curiosity and raise issues. With the exception of Chapter 13, all Focus pages are based on primary source material from the Roman world. On occasion, the original source has been transposed into a modern context in order to add interest. Sources for the Focus pages are given in the Teachers' Guide.

2. **The Sources**
    All written sources which appear in the main body of each chapter are translated paraphrases of the original Latin or Greek. The language has been adapted to aid comprehension.

    All original artwork is based on primary source material - either literary or archaeological.

3. **The Teachers' Guide**
    A teachers' guide is available. It is photocopiable and provides assessment tests, guidance for marking, advice for teaching, additional information and worksheets with further activities including games and simulations.

CONTENTS

INTRODUCTION

In the beginning

The early history of Rome is lost in the mists of time. All that is left is a legend. It goes like this.

Rome was founded in 753 BC by Romulus and Remus, twin sons of the god Mars. As babies, the twins were abandoned in a cradle on the banks of the River Tiber. A she-wolf found them and fed them with her milk. Some time later a shepherd stumbled across the twins, took them home and brought them up as his own children. When they grew up they built a town on the spot where they had been found. Soon after this, they had an argument and Romulus killed his brother. The new town was named Rome after its first King – Romulus.

A legend is a mixture of fact and fiction – a story which is partly true and partly made up. Much of Roman history is like this. It is the job of the modern historian to sort out what is accurate and what is invented.

Source A

Romulus and Remus and the she-wolf

Source B   Plan of Rome

Activities

1. Which parts of the story of Romulus and Remus do you think are true and which are not?

2. a) What is happening in Source A?

   b) Why do you think a Roman artist chose to make a sculpture of this scene?

3. Look at Source B. Why was this a good place to build a town?

4. Put the following dates in order starting with the earliest. AD 14, 504 BC, AD 126, 210 BC, 54 BC.

Did you know?

Modern dates give the number of the year and say whether it is BC or AD. BC stands for 'Before Christ's Birth' and AD stands for 'After Christ's Birth'.

So, AD 1900 means 1900 years after Christ's birth. It was the beginning of the twentieth century. 100 BC means 100 years before Christ's birth and was the beginning of the first century BC.

The Empire

At first the Roman government only ruled the area around Rome. But as time went on, Rome ruled a larger and larger area made up of countries it had conquered. When one country rules a number of other countries, this is known as an Empire.

The Roman Empire grew slowly and it was won by war. At first the Roman army fought against other cities in Italy. Later it fought against enemies further from home.

As the Empire grew so did Rome itself, from a small town to a splendid city. Wooden houses were rebuilt in stone and decorated with marble. Victorious generals built temples and arches. The centre of Rome became a place full of grand buildings and monuments to the city's heroes. Eventually, more than a million people lived in this one city – a huge population compared to other cities in the ancient world.

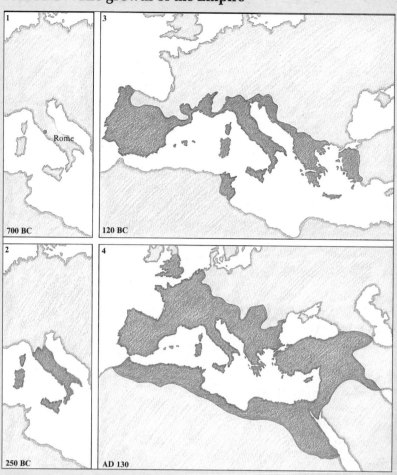

Source C   The growth of the Empire

1   Rome   700 BC

2   250 BC

3   120 BC

4   AD 130

Activities

1. Look at Source C and explain what it shows.

2. Draw an outline of the Empire shown in Map 4. Mark on the names of modern countries. You can use an atlas to help you.

3. Source D is drawn by a modern artist.

   a) What evidence do you think the artist used to make this picture as accurate as possible?

   b) How does it differ from a modern city centre?

Source D

Ancient Rome – city centre

Evidence

You are on holiday in North Wales playing in a stream which runs down from a hill called Dinas. The sun glints on a shiny object in the water. It is round and silver with a man's head on one side and some marks which look like writing. You notice a farmer in a nearby field and walk over. 'That's a Roman coin,' he tells you. 'Quite a few have been found in this stream. The Romans used to have a fort on the hill.'

Next day you take the coin to a museum. You get quite excited when they tell you about your find. 'Yes, that's a Roman coin. The marks are writing. It's in Latin, the language spoken by the Romans. The man on the coin is the Emperor Hadrian. He died in AD 138.'

What you've found is **evidence** about Roman history. From this one piece of evidence you've learned a lot – the Romans had coins, at least some of them could read and write, they used metal, they probably came to Wales, they were ruled by Emperors, they lived a long time ago.

You've done some good detective work. You've found clues which have helped you to uncover the past. Historians work in much the same way. They gather evidence which provides clues about what happened in the past.

Source A

Part of the writings of the Roman historian Tacitus copied in the eleventh century.

Source B   The Emperor Hadrian

Written evidence

Historians studying the Roman Empire use two main types of evidence – written records and archaeological remains. Luckily a large amount of written material from Roman times has survived – usually copies made by monks in the Middle Ages. It includes histories of Rome written by Roman historians, letters from Emperors and Governors of the provinces and poems, plays and stories by Roman authors.

This book contains many examples of written evidence for you to study. But don't believe everything you read. Written evidence may not be accurate. It is often one-sided, giving only one point of view. It may be a legend like the story of Romulus and Remus. Written evidence must be 'handled with care'.

Source C   Roman pottery

Archaeological evidence

Archaeological evidence is the remains left by people in the past. These remains are found and examined by archaeologists.

Archaeological evidence from Roman times includes things that the Romans made – such as coins, pottery, statues and buildings. It also includes things that the Romans used – such as walnut shells, fish skeletons, goats' teeth and snail shells, all of which have been found in Roman rubbish pits.

By using both written and archaeological evidence, it is often possible to find out a great deal about life in the Roman world. The two types of evidence can be used to check each other. For example a piece of written evidence might tell us that the Romans invaded Britain in AD 43. But unless we have also found archaeological remains which show this, we cannot be sure that the written evidence is true.

Source D

Model of a Roman farmhouse. It is based on remains found at Fishbourne in Sussex.

Source E

Part of the Roman town of Pompeii in Italy. In AD 79 Pompeii was completely buried after Mount Vesuvius erupted.

Activities

1. Explain why historians need to use both written records and archaeological remains. What are the problems if only one type of evidence is available?

2. Rubbish pits are just as important as statues to archaeologists. What can be learned from each type of evidence?

3. What do Sources B–E tell us about life in the Roman world?

4. Suppose that your school had been abandoned 1500 years ago and only ruins were left.

   a) Draw a plan of the remains of the buildings.

   b) How might an archaeologist discover that the buildings had been used as a school?

   c) What sorts of things would survive for 1500 years and what would not?

2

THE REPUBLIC

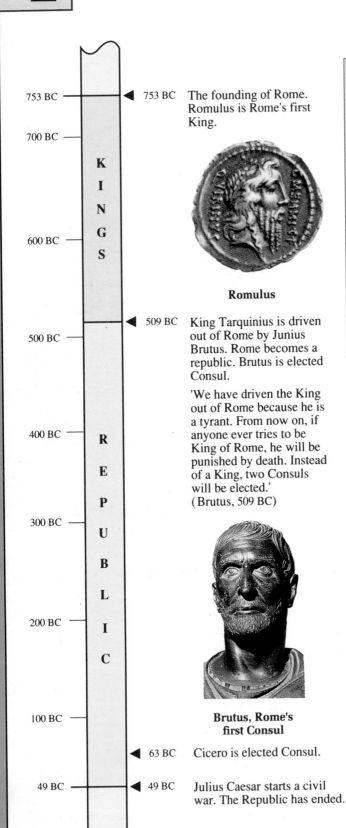

753 BC ◀ 753 BC The founding of Rome. Romulus is Rome's first King.

Romulus

509 BC ◀ 509 BC King Tarquinius is driven out of Rome by Junius Brutus. Rome becomes a republic. Brutus is elected Consul.

'We have driven the King out of Rome because he is a tyrant. From now on, if anyone ever tries to be King of Rome, he will be punished by death. Instead of a King, two Consuls will be elected.' (Brutus, 509 BC)

Brutus, Rome's first Consul

63 BC ◀ 63 BC Cicero is elected Consul.

49 BC ◀ 49 BC Julius Caesar starts a civil war. The Republic has ended.

Themes

At first, Rome was ruled by Kings. Roman historians tell us that there were seven Kings in all. They ruled Rome for nearly 250 years.

But in 509 BC the seventh King, Tarquinius Superbus, was forced to leave Rome forever. The people, led by Junius Brutus, had had enough. Tarquinius was a cruel ruler who cared for nobody. The people decided that Rome would never be ruled by Kings again.

So, in 509 BC Rome became a republic. A republic is a country that does not have a King at its head. The Roman Republic lasted for more than 450 years. It was ruled by two leaders, known as Consuls, and a Senate made up of 600 Senators who were elected by the citizens of Rome.

This chapter looks at the following questions.

- How did the Roman Republic work?
- Who had power and who did not?

We begin with a view of the Republic from one of Rome's most famous Senators and Consuls, Marcus Tullius Cicero. The interview on the Focus page is based on a book called *The Republic* which was written by Cicero in 51 BC.

Focus Activities

1. You are one of the two Consuls. Explain what you would do if you wanted to make a new law.

2. Why were Consuls elected for one year only?

3. Does Cicero think that the Republic is a good type of government? Explain how you know.

Book of the Year 51 BC

The winner of the Book of the Year award for 51 BC is *The Republic* by Marcus Tullius Cicero. The author is also an important Senator. We visited him at his home and asked him to explain how this 'Republic' works.

Interviewer	At first, Rome was ruled by Kings. Why don't we have Kings now?
Cicero	It didn't work. Some Kings became tyrants.
Interviewer	What do you mean by 'tyrants'?
Cicero	A tyrant is a cruel ruler who doesn't listen to anyone else. The last King, Tarquinius Superbus, was a tyrant. He refused to listen to the Senate or to the people. And that's why he was thrown out of Rome and why Rome became a republic.
Interviewer	So, if there is no King in Rome, who's in charge?
Cicero	The Consuls. Each year, the Roman citizens elect two Senators as Consuls for one year, and one year only. The next year two different Senators are elected as Consuls. This makes sure that no one has power for too long. If people did have power for too long they might turn into tyrants.
Interviewer	You say that the Consuls are Senators. Who are these Senators and what do they do?
Cicero	Senators are the richest and wisest men in Rome. Their job is to give advice to the Consuls. When a Consul wants to make a new law, he first calls for a meeting of the Senate and the Senators discuss the new law.
Interviewer	What happens then?
Cicero	If the Senators agree to the new law, the Consuls call the citizens to an Assembly where a vote is taken on it. If the citizens vote 'yes', the law has been passed and must be obeyed.
Interviewer	So, the Roman citizens have two jobs. They vote to elect the Consuls and also vote for or against new laws?
Cicero	Yes, and that is why the Republic will never be ruled by tyrants.
Interviewer	Marcus Tullius Cicero, thank you.

Cicero

Governing the Republic

When people live and work together they have rules which everybody must obey. For example, every school has rules which must be obeyed by its pupils. The same is true of a country.

A country's rules are known as laws. But who makes the laws? The answer is the government.

The Roman Republic lasted for more than 450 years. During this period, three main groups of people were involved in making laws. Together they made up the government. They were:

- The Senate
- The Consuls
- The Assemblies of Roman citizens

Source A   The Senate

The Senate was a group of about 600 men whose job was to give advice to the Consuls. New laws and political problems were discussed by the Senate.

In some ways, the Senate was like the House of Commons. For example, its members were elected by the people and they were full-time politicians. However, in other ways the Senate was very different from the House of Commons. For example:

- Senators were Senators for life. They did not have to be re-elected like Members of Parliament.
- Only men were allowed to be Senators.
- Senators had to be very rich.
- There were no political parties in the Senate.

This picture shows a meeting of the Senate. Senators wore special purple bordered robes called togas. The meeting was chaired by one of the Consuls.

Source B   The Consuls

Every year two members of the Senate were elected as Consuls. Together they were in charge of government. The two Consuls took it in turns to carry out their duties. Each was in charge for one month at a time.

The Consuls had many duties. These included:

- Calling meetings of the Senate
- Chairing these meetings
- Suggesting new laws
- Organising elections
- Commanding the army
- Performing religious ceremonies
- Meeting ambassadors from foreign countries

Statue of a Consul with the heads of his ancestors

Source C   The Assemblies

An Assembly was a special meeting of Roman citizens. The citizens gathered in a field just outside Rome and were asked to vote.

Assemblies were called for two reasons:

1. **Elections**

   Citizens voted for the new Consuls and new Senators.

2. **New Laws**

   Citizens voted 'yes' or 'no' depending on whether they agreed with a new law or not.

Citizens were only allowed to vote if they went to the Assembly in person.

The rich had more votes than other citizens. This meant that they usually got their own way.

Activities

1. In what ways were Senators different from Members of Parliament?
2. Do you think Consuls would pay attention to what the citizens wanted? Explain your answer.
3. Why do you think there were two Consuls rather than one?
4. Ordinary Roman citizens had an important part to play in the government of the Republic. Explain why.

Citizens and non-citizens

By the time that Cicero published his book *The Republic* in 51 BC, Rome ruled a huge Empire (see p. 5). More than ten million people lived in this Empire. But only a small percentage were Roman citizens – there were about one million citizens in 70 BC.

A Roman citizen was a free man (that is, not a slave) who was born in Rome. A citizen's sons were also Roman citizens. Non-citizens fell into three groups – women, slaves and people born in the provinces (the lands conquered by Rome).

Non-citizens were not allowed to stand for election to become a Consul or a Senator. Nor were they allowed to vote in Assemblies. Non-citizens made up a large percentage of the people who lived in the Roman Empire. They had no political power.

Source A Slaves

Slave cleaning a boot

Most Roman citizens owned slaves. A slave was a person's property just like a house or a piece of furniture. Slaves had no political power.

Slaves could buy their freedom – if their owner allowed them to do so. If slaves did buy their freedom, they themselves did not become Roman citizens but their sons did.

Source B Women

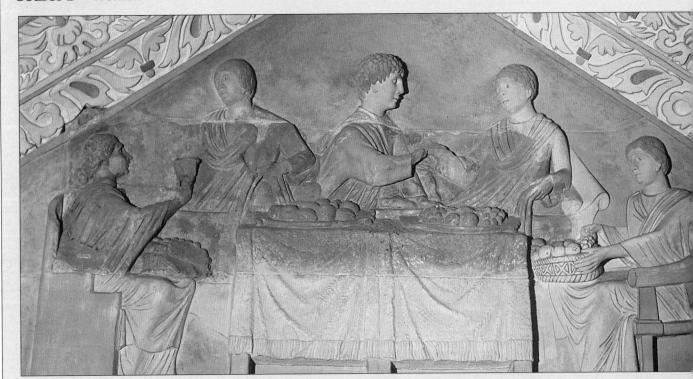

No woman was a full Roman citizen. Women, therefore, did not have any political power.

Source C People born in the provinces

Lucius Cornelius Balbus was born in Spain which was a Roman province. Like all people born in the provinces whose parents were not citizens Balbus was born a non-citizen, though he did come from a wealthy family.

Balbus worked hard for Rome and became even wealthier. He got to know important Romans, including some Senators. In 72 BC he was rewarded for his services to Rome by a special grant of citizenship. Thirty-two years later Balbus became Consul.

Once Balbus became a Roman citizen he had a number of advantages: he could vote at Assemblies and stand for election; he was protected by Roman law; and he did not have to pay tax if he lived in Italy.

Balbus' story is important for two reasons. First, it shows us that people who were born in the provinces were not Roman citizens unless they were given citizenship as a special reward. Second, it shows us that it was possible for a new citizen to rise right to the top in Roman politics.

A special coin with the name of Balbus written on it and a picture of a club. The club stands for the town of Gades in Spain where Balbus was born. This coin told everybody that Balbus was an important Senator.

Activities

1. 'The Republic was a good system of government because the people had some say in the way they were ruled.' Is this true? Explain your answer.

2. Why do you think women, slaves and most people born in the provinces were not allowed to have political power?

3. You were born in a province but have just been given Roman citizenship. Why should that make you happy?

Checklist

- From 753 to 509 BC, Rome was ruled by Kings. It then became a republic.

- The three main parts of the government were the Senate, the Consuls and the Assemblies.

- Power was not shared equally. Rich citizens had most political power. Those without a vote – women, slaves and people born in the provinces – had least.

- The Roman Republic lasted for more than 450 years.

3

JULIUS CAESAR

Julius Caesar

Themes

On the 15th March 44 BC Julius Caesar was stabbed to death at a meeting of the Senate. For nine months he alone had ruled Rome. A group of Senators made secret plans to murder him. They believed that Caesar wanted to become King of Rome and the only way to prevent this was to kill him.

The previous chapter examined the government of the Republic. It was designed to prevent one man from gaining too much power. Many Senators believed that Julius Caesar was now too powerful and must be stopped.

This chapter looks at the following questions.

- How did Caesar come to power?

- What had happened to make Senators believe that Caesar aimed to become a King?

- What would happen once Caesar was dead? Would the Republic survive?

Focus Activities

Of course there were no newspapers in ancient Rome. If there had been, then the front page on the day after Caesar was killed might have looked something like the page opposite.

Suppose you were a reporter following Caesar around on the day of his death. Use the information on the Focus page to write a report which explains:

a) what happened on the morning before Caesar was killed;

b) how people reacted when he was stabbed;

c) why Caesar was murdered.

Caesar murdered in Senate: Rome shocked

by Gaius Suetonius Tranquillus

The Roman world is stunned. At about 2 o'clock yesterday afternoon, Julius Caesar was brutally murdered during a meeting of the Senate. Minutes after he arrived at the meeting, Caesar was surrounded by a group of Senators. They drew daggers and stabbed him to death. Chaos followed and Caesar's bloodstained body was left lying at the foot of Pompey's statue, riddled with stab wounds.

CONSPIRACY!

First reports from the scene of the crime suggest that a group of Senators had made secret plans to kill Caesar. There was, in other words, a conspiracy and, no doubt, history will remember those Senators who killed Caesar as 'the conspirators'. An eye-witness said, 'The Senator who led the attack on Caesar was Brutus. He and the others walked calmly out of the meeting waving their daggers in the air. They kept shouting "The tyrant is dead! Long live the Republic, long live freedom".'

COUNTDOWN TO MURDER

The night before Caesar and his wife Calpurnia both have nightmares.

6am Caesar gets up and has breakfast.

7am Caesar begins writing letters and his speech.

9.30am Calpurnia does not want Caesar to go out because of bad omens (signs).

10am Caesar agrees not to leave, but is then persuaded not to disappoint the Senate by Decimus Brutus (one of the conspirators).

10.15am Caesar leaves his house and is surrounded by supporters. One man gives Caesar a note which reveals the plot against him. Caesar puts it at the bottom of a pile of papers and walks slowly through Rome discussing business.

1.15pm Caesar goes into the Senate House.

1.20pm Tillius Cimber approaches Caesar with a letter. A group of Senators crowd round him.

1.22pm Cimber grabs Caesar. Other Senators draw daggers and stab him. Caesar pulls his toga (robe) over his head and remains silent. Brutus stabs him. Caesar groans, and falls down dead.

1.25pm Panic in the Senate House. Conspirators walk out in a group. Other Senators run away.

2pm Examination of his body is carried out by Caesar's Greek doctor, Antistius. He finds 23 stab wounds.

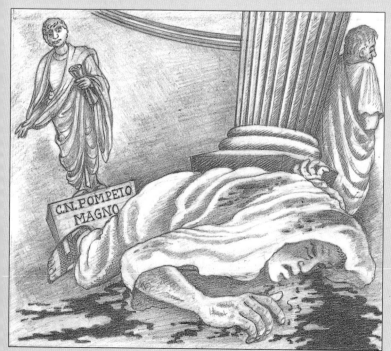

C.N. POMPEIO MAGNO

Caesar lies dead in the Senate House

The decline of the Republic

Julius Caesar was born in 100 BC and died in 44 BC. During his lifetime, the government of the Republic started to break down. People began to have different views about how Rome should be ruled (Sources A and C). Supporters of these different views often ended up fighting each other (Source B).

Every Senator wanted to be Consul. Every Senator wanted to win battles and become famous. Every Senator wanted others to support his views. In the last years of the Republic, this competition between Senators led to civil war (war between citizens of the same country).

Source A Sallust's view of government

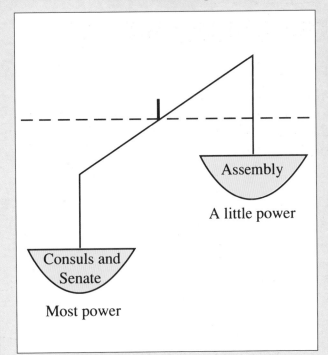

Some Senators believed that the Consuls and the Senate had too much power. They wanted the Assemblies to have a bigger say in the way Rome was ruled. These Senators worked hard to win the support of ordinary citizens.

Source B Lucius Cornelius Sulla

The first man to start a civil war was the Consul Sulla. In 87 BC he marched on Rome with his army and won power by force. Although he soon retired and the normal government of the Republic continued, Sulla's actions would not be forgotten.

Source C Cicero's view of government

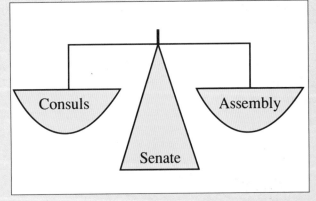

Some Senators believed that the Consuls and the Senate had the right amount of power. They thought that the government of the Republic was balanced and should not be changed. They looked down on ordinary citizens and argued that the Senators who supported them really wanted power for themselves.

Caesar – the road to power

Julius Caesar was 21 when Sulla retired. He saw how Sulla had won power by force. He also saw that after Sulla retired nothing really changed.

When Caesar became a Senator, he worked hard to gain the support of the ordinary citizens. He gave land to the poor and stood up for their rights. He also became popular because he was an excellent general. In the Senate he got other Senators to support him by making secret agreements with them.

But Caesar soon made enemies. Some powerful Senators did not like his methods or his popularity. They worked against him.

The result was civil war. In 49 BC Caesar led his army from Gaul into Italy and marched on Rome (see Source D). He was determined to win power by force and he would not make the same mistake as Sulla by retiring.

The civil war lasted four years. Caesar defeated his enemies. By 45 BC he was in control of the whole Roman Empire.

Source D   Caesar's career

BC

100 Born. His father was a Consul and his family was very wealthy.

67 Already a successful soldier, Caesar is elected to the Senate.

61 Wins an important war in Spain.

60 Makes secret agreement with two powerful Senators – Pompey and Crassus. They help him get elected as Consul.

59 Elected as Consul. Falls out with the other Consul, Bibulus, who opposes changes Caesar wants to make.

58 - 49 Conquers Gaul (modern France and Belgium). Some Senators are jealous of his success and afraid because he has a large army.

55 Is the first Roman general to bring an army to Britain. Returns to Britain in 54 BC.

51 - 49 Begins a civil war against his enemies who are led by Pompey. Caesar wins. He pardons (forgives) his enemies.

45 Returns to Rome and elected ruler.

44 Murdered.

Portrait of Caesar on a coin

Activities

1. What would you think about Caesar if:
   (a) you agreed with Sallust's view of government (Source A);
   (b) you agreed with Cicero's view of government (Source C)?

2. What did Caesar learn from what Sulla had done?

3. During Caesar's lifetime there was a struggle for power. Explain why, using the information on these pages.

Caesar the ruler

After winning the civil war, Caesar was made 'ruler for life' by the Senate. No one had been ruler for life since the last King, Tarquinius Superbus.

Caesar made changes in the way Rome was ruled. His enemies did not like these changes. The Consuls were no longer elected. They were now chosen by Caesar. Caesar passed new laws without taking notice of what the Senate thought. These were important changes in the way the Republic was run.

Caesar was very popular with ordinary citizens, but the Senate was split between those who supported him and those who opposed him. His opponents believed that he aimed to become a King.

Source A   Caesar and kingship

In 45 BC, Mark Antony, the Consul, approached Caesar and tried to crown him. Caesar refused the crown each time it was offered.

Source B   Caesar and the Senate

Supporters

Caesar was a brilliant general. He never lost a war.

Caesar always encouraged people to say what they thought. No one was ever punished for speaking against him.

Caesar deserves the honours that he has been given.

Caesar was very generous – especially to ordinary people.

The best thing about Caesar is that he forgave everyone who fought against him in the civil war. He even gave his enemies in the Senate important jobs in government.

Opponents

Caesar and his friends make all the important decisions. The rest of the Senate might just as well not be there.

Caesar chooses the Consuls. That means you have to say things to please him.

Caesar forced the Senate to give him the title 'ruler for life'. He wants to be a King.

Senators are only supposed to have special powers for one year at a time.

Although Caesar forgave Senators who fought against him, they still secretly hate him.

All the comments above were made by Senators and recorded by Roman historians.

After the murder

Caesar was killed because his opponents believed he was becoming a tyrant. But once he was dead, what would happen? Those involved in the plot hoped that by killing Caesar they could go back to the republican system of government. Caesar's supporters had different ideas.

Source D shows the key events that followed Caesar's death.

Source D   Timeline 44-31 BC

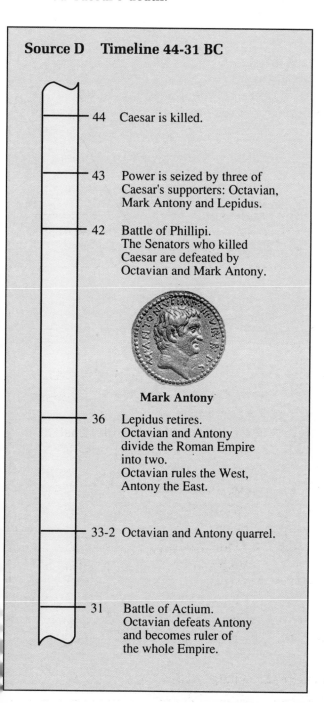

— 44   Caesar is killed.

— 43   Power is seized by three of Caesar's supporters: Octavian, Mark Antony and Lepidus.

— 42   Battle of Phillipi.
The Senators who killed Caesar are defeated by Octavian and Mark Antony.

Mark Antony

— 36   Lepidus retires.
Octavian and Antony divide the Roman Empire into two.
Octavian rules the West, Antony the East.

— 33-2   Octavian and Antony quarrel.

— 31   Battle of Actium.
Octavian defeats Antony and becomes ruler of the whole Empire.

Activities

1. Why do you think Caesar refused the crown? (Sources A and C)

2. What kind of person was Caesar according to his supporters in the Senate? (Source B)

3. Caesar's opponents wanted a return to republican government. How do we know this from Source B?

4. Caesar's murder solved nothing. It split the Roman Empire. Explain using Source D.

5. Use what you have learned in this chapter to explain why Caesar was killed in 44 BC.

Checklist

- Caesar's career was a turning point in Roman history. It marked the end of the Republic.

- The Senators who killed Caesar believed that Caesar aimed to be King and the only way to stop this was to kill him.

- After Caesar's death there was another civil war between those who had supported him and those who opposed him.

THE PRINCIPATE

Emperor

Consuls

Senate

Ordinary citizens

Non-citizens

The Principate

Augustus (Octavian), the first Emperor

Themes

By winning the Battle of Actium in 31 BC, Octavian won power for himself. He was now ruler of the whole Roman Empire.

Octavian wanted to remain ruler, but he did not want to make the mistake that his uncle Julius Caesar had made. Caesar had been killed because some Senators thought he was becoming a King. Octavian wanted to keep the power he had won, but he did not want to appear to be a King. Therefore, he tried to hide his power. In doing so he invented a new system of government.

The new system of government is known as the Principate. It was headed by a man who was ruler for life – the Emperor. Octavian was the first Emperor. This chapter looks at the Principate and asks:

- What did it mean to be Emperor?

- How did the Principate work?

It is 28 BC. Octavian has ruled Rome for nearly four years. People are beginning to grumble that it is time for a return to republican government.

Focus Activities

The page from the diary shown opposite is not a real historical document. But a meeting of the Senate really did take place in January, 27 BC. The Senators really did make these decisions. It was at this meeting that Octavian's reign as Emperor officially began.

You were one of the Senators at the meeting. Another Senator - a friend of yours - could not go because he was abroad. Write a letter to him which explains why the meeting was so important and why the Senators agreed to do what Octavian wanted.

The diary of Gaius Julius Caesar Octavianus

December, 28 BC

Dear diary

I have a problem. It is now almost four years since I won the Battle of Actium and became ruler of the Roman Empire. But if I'm not careful people will think that I want to be King – and you know what happened to my uncle Julius when people got that idea. The trouble is that I do not want to retire. If I did there would only be civil war all over again.

Well, I've thought about it long and hard. I've talked to my friends in the Senate. Here's what we plan to do.

I'm going to call a meeting of the Senate at the beginning of January, 27 BC. During the meeting I shall say that I am giving up all my powers and retiring. 'We are going back to the Republic,' I shall say. This should cause quite a stir. But then my friend Agrippa will make a speech. He'll thank me for all that I have done for Rome. He'll say that I am too

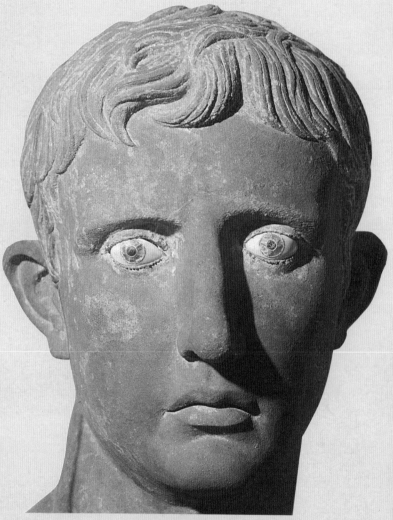

Augustus (Octavian)

valuable to be allowed to retire – after all, I am only 35 years old. Then he'll say, 'If you will not be ruler on your own, will you at least help us to rule?' When he says this, I shall look modestly at the floor and he will say, 'Senators, don't let Octavian retire. Let us give him special powers.' Of course, the Senators will agree to this and, in reality, I will still be in charge. But everyone will think that I don't really want all this power. They'll think that I am modest and that I had to be forced not to retire. No one will ever think that I want to be King.

Then, after that has been agreed, Agrippa will suggest that I am given a special title – Augustus. From that day on, no one will call me Octavian. I shall be Augustus. You see, a new name shows that there is a new beginning.

The Principate

The Principate was different from the Republic because in the Principate one man had power and he had power for life. This man was known as the Emperor.

The main reason why the Emperor had power was because he was in charge of the army. Soldiers swore an oath of loyalty to Augustus and to all the Emperors who followed him. It was the loyalty of the army which gave an Emperor his power.

Although the Emperor had power, the system of government in the Principate did not look very different from that in the Republic. There were still two Consuls each year and there was still a Senate. But in the Principate, the Consuls and the Senate did what the Emperor wanted them to do. The Emperor made all the important decisions.

Source A   Augustus as a general

The Emperor was the commander of the army and he paid their wages.

Source B   The first Emperors

AUGUSTUS
b. 63 BC; r. 27 BC-AD 14;
d. - natural

TIBERIUS
b. 42 BC; r. AD 14-37;
d. - natural

GAIUS (CALIGULA)
b. AD 12; r. AD 37-41;
d. - murdered by Senators

CLAUDIUS
b. 10 BC; r. AD 41-54;
d. - natural

NERO
b. AD 37; r. AD 54-68;
d. - suicide

b. = born; r. = years of reign; d. = type of death

In the Republic, Consuls made the important decisions with the help of the Senate. These decisions were then taken to the Assemblies and the Assemblies voted 'yes' or 'no'. In the Principate there were no Assemblies.

The Emperor chose which Senators could stand for election as Consuls and two of them were elected each year by the Senate. The Emperor made all the important decisions in private, with the help of a group of advisors.

Once a decision had been made, the Emperor ordered a meeting of the Senate. The Senate had a discussion and voted 'yes' or 'no'. In fact, the Senate hardly ever voted 'no' to a decision made by the Emperor. Most were scared that if they voted 'no', the Emperor would not choose them to be Consul or help them in other ways.

Source C   An Emperor and his advisors

This picture shows the Emperor Claudius discussing a new law with his advisors. His advisors are Senators. The meeting takes place in the Emperor's home – the Imperial palace in Rome.

Activities

1. Why do you think that the Emperors insisted that soldiers swore an oath of loyalty to them?

2. Use the information in Source B to work out how old each Emperor was at the beginning of his reign. Then draw a timeline, marking on the reigns of the five Emperors.

3. How were important decisions made in the Principate?

The Emperor and the Senate

The Focus page shows that Octavian (Augustus) tricked the Senate. He had learned from what had happened to Julius Caesar. He cleverly tried to hide his real power. He did this by pretending that Rome had gone back to the Republic. As a result of this trick, the Senate continued to meet as it had done in the Republic. But it no longer had any real power because the important decisions were made by the Emperor.

Despite this, in the Principate, the Senate still had an important part to play in government. Although the Emperor was in charge, he still needed people to help him rule. These people came from the Senate.

The trouble was that Senators did not want to upset the Emperor. Also the Senators did not always know what was going on.

Source A The Emperor Tiberius and the Senate AD 23

Adapted from Tacitus

Source B The Emperor Tiberius and the Senate AD 14

Adapted from Tacitus

Dynasty

An Emperor was Emperor for life. But what happened when he died?

In the Republic, this question did not arise because people did not have power for life. But in the Principate, this was an important question.

What happened was that the first Emperor, Augustus, decided that he wanted a member of his family to become the next Emperor.

When power is passed from one member of a family to another, this is called a dynasty.

The first five Emperors were all related to each other. Source C shows how they were related.

The first five Emperors are known as the Julio-Claudian dynasty. Other dynasties followed this one.

Source C   Family tree of the Julio-Claudian Emperors

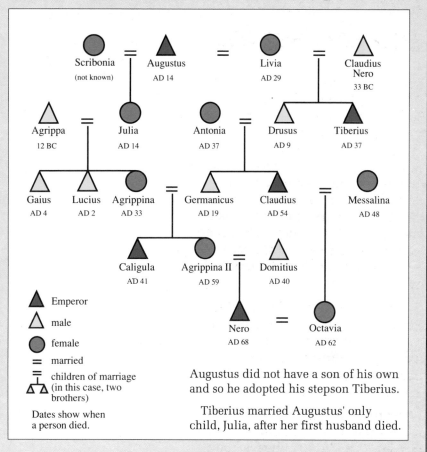

Augustus did not have a son of his own and so he adopted his stepson Tiberius.

Tiberius married Augustus' only child, Julia, after her first husband died.

Activities

1. Why does Source A suggest that the Senate did not have much power?

2. Explain what is happening in Source B. What does the Emperor think of the Senators and why?

3. Caligula, Claudius and Nero were directly related to Augustus and/or Tiberius. Use Source C to explain how they were related.

4. You are a Roman who lived in both the Republic and the Principate. Write a letter to your friend in Greece explaining the differences between the two systems of government.

Checklist

- From 27 BC, Rome was ruled by a new system of government known as the Principate.

- The Emperor's real power came from his control of the army.

- All important decisions were made by the Emperor in secret.

- The Senate continued to meet but it had no real power. The Senators hardly ever opposed the wishes of the Emperor.

- Augustus created a dynasty. The next four Emperors were all related to him. Other dynasties followed this one.

THE ARMY AND INVASION

Roman soldiers fighting against a Germanic tribe

Themes

War had always played an important part in Roman life. To begin with, the Romans fought against their neighbours to protect their own city. As time went on they fought further and further from home. In AD 43 the Romans decided to invade Britain.

Warfare in Roman times was very different from warfare today. Soldiers fought with spears and swords. The main part of a battle was a bit like a rugby scrum with everybody piling in. Usually one side would panic and run away. Roman soldiers hardly ever panicked. They were well trained and well organised.

This chapter looks at the following questions.

- How was the Roman army organised and what were its soldiers like?

- Why did the Romans invade Britain in AD 43?

- Apart from fighting, what else did the Roman army do?

Our starting point is AD 43. The new Emperor Claudius has sent an army to conquer Britain.

Focus Activities

1. Make THREE copies of the map on the Focus page. Use one map for each part of the question.

    Using the key shown on the map, show the position of the soldiers:

    a) at the start of the battle;

    b) when the Batavians attacked the chariots;

    c) just before the British made their final attack on the Romans.

2. Why did the Romans win this battle?

The Battle of the Medway, AD 43

When the Romans reached the high ground which looked out over the River Medway, the commanding officer, Aulus Plautius, ordered his men to halt. From this position Plautius could see that the British army was lined up on the opposite bank of the river. He decided that this was where the battle would take place.

Plautius realised that it was important to take the Britons by surprise. This would not be difficult. The Britons had not fought against the Romans since Caesar came to Britain in 55 and 54 BC, so they did not know very much about the Romans' methods of fighting. Also, the Britons did not know that the Romans had special troops – 'Batavians' – who were trained to swim across rivers in full armour.

The plan was a clever one. The main part of the Roman army marched down the hill. They stopped on the bank of the river opposite the Britons. Then they made it look as if they were getting ready to attack. While the Britons were watching this, the Batavians went downstream where the river was wider and swam across it. Once across, they made for the chariots parked behind and alongside the British troops. The Britons turned to defend their chariots. It was too late. The Batavians killed or wounded most of the horses that pulled the chariots. The Britons could not use their main weapon.

In the meantime, the main part of the Roman army marched upstream and crossed the river where it was narrow. The Britons were too busy defending their chariots to notice. Once on the same side of the river as the Britons, the Roman soldiers got into position and waited for the Britons to attack them. When the attack came, the Romans stood firm and beat back the British troops.

The plan worked. The Britons were easily defeated. South East Britain was under Roman control and would remain so for over 350 years.

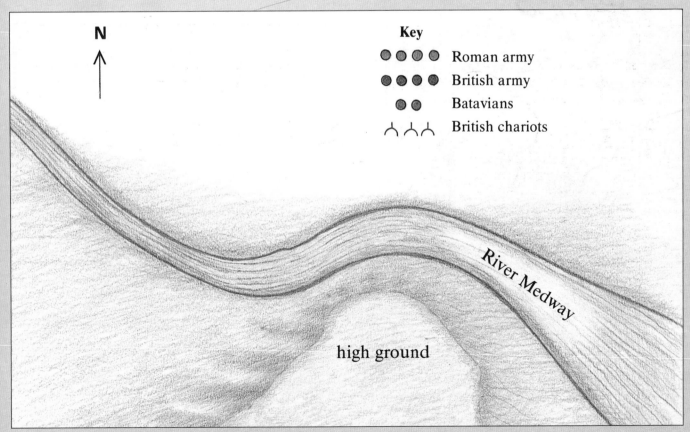

A plan of the battle site

The invasion of Britain

Julius Caesar was the first Roman general to go to Britain. He went there with his army in 55 and 54 BC.

Before Caesar went, the Romans were not sure that Britain even existed. Many Romans believed that Britain was a magical island full of fabulous wealth and inhabited by monsters. It was only after Caesar's visit that the Romans could be sure that Britain was a real island and that the people who lived there were just like people who lived anywhere else.

Between 54 BC and AD 43, the Roman army did not go back to Britain. Roman traders, though, did visit. Some tribes began to trade with the Romans and some made friendly agreements with the Roman government. Other tribes, however, became enemies of Rome. The tribes used their coins to show whether they were friends or enemies of Rome (see Source B).

Source A   A Briton

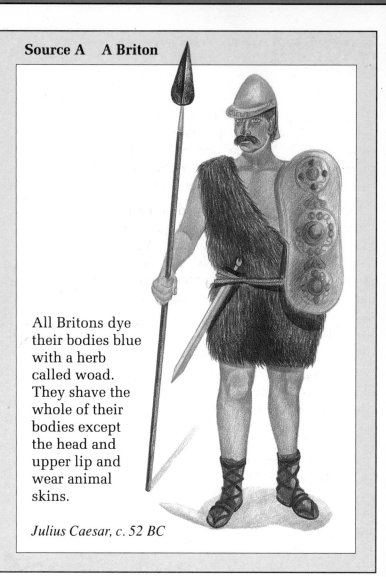

All Britons dye their bodies blue with a herb called woad. They shave the whole of their bodies except the head and upper lip and wear animal skins.

Julius Caesar, c. 52 BC

Source B   British coins

This coin shows a bunch of grapes. Grapes were used to make wine. Grapes and wine were unknown in Britain before the Romans visited. The tribe using this coin was a friend of Rome.

This coin shows a stalk of barley. Barley was used to make beer. Beer was drunk in Britain long before the Romans visited. The tribe using this coin was an enemy of Rome.

Why did Claudius invade Britain?

Claudius was related to Augustus. Therefore, he had the right family background to become Emperor. But he was born with a limp and a stutter and so no one thought he would ever become Emperor.

Until AD 41 Claudius stayed at home studying. Then everything changed. The Emperor Caligula was murdered. A group of soldiers found Claudius hiding in a cupboard in the Imperial palace and said he should be Emperor. People came out onto the streets to support him. Claudius became Emperor.

Once Claudius was Emperor, he had to prove that he was the man for the job. He decided that the best way to do this was to invade Britain. He chose Britain because it was far away and he knew he would be admired for invading new and dangerous lands. Also, Claudius knew that his army would have little trouble beating the Britons. If successful, Claudius would be seen to be a great leader.

Claudius' invasion was successful. He reigned for another eleven years until he died aged 64.

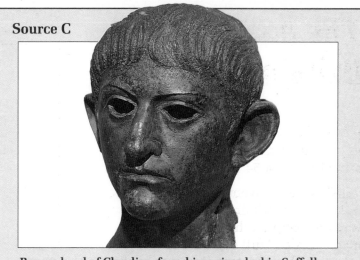

Source C

Bronze head of Claudius, found in a river bed in Suffolk

Source D   The Roman invasion

Area of conquest
Frontier zone
Battle
River Medway
1 Boulogne
2 Richborough
3 London
4 St Albans
5 Colchester
6 Lincoln
7 Exeter

9th Legion

14th Legion   20th Legion

2nd Legion

Activities

1. Before 55 BC many Romans believed that Britain was a magical island. Why might the Roman soldiers have thought that this was true when they first landed in Britain in 55 BC? (Use Source A.)

2. Explain why each of the designs on the coins in Source B was a good way to show that the tribe was either a friend or an enemy of the Romans.

3. Using Source C write a description of Claudius. Does he look like an Emperor?

4. Use Source D to explain what happened during the invasion of Britain.

The Roman army

The Roman army was very well organised. It was divided into legions. From the reign of Augustus there were 28 legions, each containing about 5500 soldiers (legionaries). Men were only allowed to be legionaries if they were Roman citizens.

Each legion was divided into 10 cohorts and each cohort was divided into 6 centuries. Each century was commanded by an officer called a centurion. Senior officers gave orders to centurions and they passed them on to the legionaries in their century. This system worked well. The Roman army was well known for its good discipline.

Legionaries stayed in the army for 20 years. They were trained to march 30 kilometres a day, to build camps and to use their spears and swords.

Did you know?

- A legionary carried his own equipment on a march. He carried a pickaxe, saw, bucket, cooking pots and food – as well as his weapons and armour.

- In war, soldiers mainly ate hard biscuits, bacon and cheese. They drank wine.

- Most orders in camp and in battle were given by blasts on the trumpet.

Source A   A Roman legionary

The style of armour and weapons changed over time. This style is from the 1st century AD.

Source B

27 legionaries in 'tortoise' formation. This was used on the approach to an enemy town or in a narrow valley. Sometimes a huge 'tortoise' was made to protect the whole army.

Auxiliaries and the cavalry

Legionaries were Roman citizens. But non-citizens could join the army as auxiliaries. Like legionaries, auxiliaries were organised into cohorts and centuries.

There were as many auxiliaries in the Roman army as there were legionaries. But auxiliaries fought with different weapons and had different armour.

Auxiliaries came from all over the Roman Empire and brought their special skills and weapons with them. Some specialised in archery or using slings. The Batavians mentioned on the Focus page were skilled at swimming in full armour. Some auxiliaries fought on horseback and are known as cavalry.

Source C   **An auxiliary soldier**

Source D

A cavalry soldier. The cavalry was the weakest part of the Roman army. Their main use was in scouting and following the enemy as it fled.

Did you know?

- Auxiliaries were paid less than legionaries.

- After 25 years' service auxiliaries were rewarded by being made Roman citizens.

- The cavalry did not have stirrups. This meant that it was easy for the rider to fall off his horse.

Activities

1. Compare Sources A and C. Make a list of the similarities and differences.

2. Look at Source B. Why would legionaries use this formation?

3. Using the information on these pages, say why you think the army was so successful in battle.

Soldiers as engineers

The army did not spend all its time fighting. After an invasion soldiers spent much of their time building. As soon as the fighting was over they built forts. They built roads and bridges to connect these forts. This helped the movement of soldiers and supplies.

Modern machines save time and work. One bulldozer can do the work of fifty people in half the time. But the Roman army had plenty of people to do the work. A legion had 5500 men. Imagine all these men building a road – the job would soon be done.

The Roman army also contained skilled engineers. The fact that Roman monuments still stand today shows this.

These pages look at one of the most famous examples of Roman military engineering – Hadrian's wall.

Hadrian was the first Emperor to decide that the Empire was big enough. Previous Emperors had not marked out the borders because they thought that Rome would go on until it conquered the whole world. Hadrian, though, ordered a wall to be built across the north of Britain from coast to coast. This marked the northern boundary of the Empire.

Source A

Hadrian's wall, near Housesteads fort

Source B

Hadrian went to Britain where he put many things right. Whilst he was there, he ordered work to begin on a wall which was to be 80 miles long and was designed to separate the Romans from the barbarians (people outside the Roman Empire).

Aelius Spartianus, c. AD 390

(This is the only piece of written evidence which mentions the building of Hadrian's wall.)

Source C   Map and plan of Hadrian's wall

turret   fort   milecastle   wall

Hadrian's wall

London

	Fort	– housed 500 or 1000 men – 16 forts in all
	Milecastle	– housed 30 men – 80 milecastles in all
	Turret	– housed 10 men – 160 turrets in all

Source D   Cross-section of Hadrian's wall

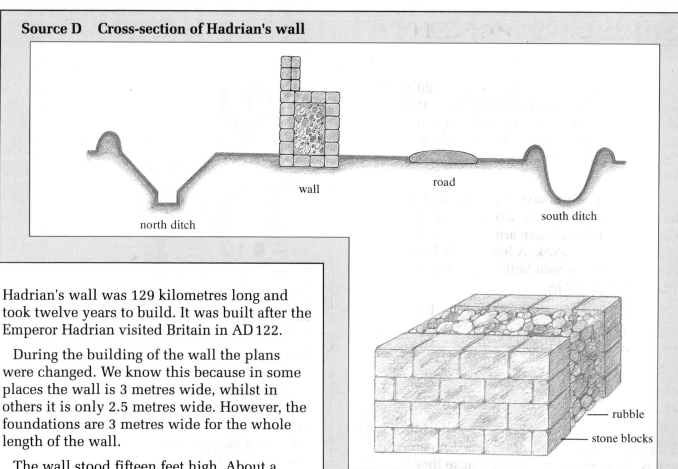

north ditch

wall

road

south ditch

rubble

stone blocks

Hadrian's wall was 129 kilometres long and took twelve years to build. It was built after the Emperor Hadrian visited Britain in AD 122.

During the building of the wall the plans were changed. We know this because in some places the wall is 3 metres wide, whilst in others it is only 2.5 metres wide. However, the foundations are 3 metres wide for the whole length of the wall.

The wall stood fifteen feet high. About a third of it was made out of turf rather than stone. This may have been because there was not enough stone available or it took too long to transport it. Originally, the wall was painted white so that it could be seen for miles around.

The wall was not built from one end to the other. Sections were built at different places and then joined up. We know this because inscriptions have been found saying that one legion built a section and a different legion built the next section.

Activities

1. Look at Sources A and C. Why do you think that Hadrian chose to build the wall here?

2. Source B says that the wall was built to separate the Romans from the barbarians. Do you think it would have worked? Use Sources C and D in your answer.

3. What does Source D tell us about the way in which the wall was built?

Checklist

- The Roman army was divided into legions. In the Principate there were 28 legions, each containing about 5500 Roman citizens.

- The legions were supported by non-citizen soldiers called auxiliaries.

- The army's job was not just to fight. Soldiers also worked as builders and engineers.

- Hadrian's wall is one of the most famous examples of Roman military engineering.

PROVINCIAL GOVERNMENT

AD 43 – Emperor Claudius invades Britain.

AD 122 – Emperor Hadrian orders a wall to be built in Britain. His reign came at the end of a period when the Empire had been growing quickly.

BRITAIN

GERMANY

59-49 BC – Julius Caesar conquers Gaul.

GAUL

146 BC – After fifty years of fighting in Greece and Macedonia, Rome takes control of the area and creates a new province.

67 BC – Pompey conquers Eastern Mediterranean – Bithynia, Cilicia and Syria become provinces.

NARBONESE GAUL

NEARER SPAIN

FURTHER SPAIN

CORSICA

SARDINIA

ILLYRICUM

ITALY

MACEDONIA

BITHYNIA

CAPPADOCIA

ASIA

CILICIA

S Y R I A

MAURETANIA

NUMIDIA

SICILY

GREECE

133 BC – King Attalus of Asia dies and leaves his kingdom to Rome – the new province of Asia is created.

JUDEA

203 BC – After the Second Punic War, Rome conquers Spain which is divided into two provinces.

AFRICA

CYRENAICA

EGYPT

146 BC – Rome attacks Carthage and creates the new province of Africa.

241 BC – After the First Punic War, Rome takes control of Sicily, Sardinia and Corsica –together they became the first province of the Roman Empire.

31 BC – Augustus invades Egypt and creates a new province.

Themes

Rome built an empire by invading new lands. By AD 117, the Roman Empire was huge, covering 1.75 million square miles.

It was very difficult for Rome to keep control of an area that was so big. It took a long time for orders and instructions to get from one end of the Empire to the other. So, how was the Empire ruled?

It was divided up into areas known as provinces. In charge of each of these provinces was a Governor.

- Who were these Governors and what did they do?

- What did local people think about the Romans after they had been invaded?

Focus Activities

1. What do these letters tell us about the sort of work Governors had to do?

2. You are a town councillor in Nicomedia. The Governor, Pliny, shows you the two letters and asks you to organise the fire fighting. You write a report explaining how you would do this.

   NOTE – Most houses were made of wood. The Romans did not have fire engines, but you could use buckets, ladders and wooden beaters.

3. Explain why the Emperor would not allow Pliny to set up a fire brigade.

BLACK SEA

BITHYNIA

• Nicomedia

The Emperor Trajan
Imperial Palace
Rome

Gaius Plinius
Governor's HQ
Nicomedia
Bithynia

c. June AD 111

Dear Sir

Whilst I was in another part of my province, a large fire broke out in the town of Nicomedia which destroyed many private houses and two public buildings. Apparently, it was fanned by a strong breeze.

I have made enquiries and there is no doubt that the fire would not have spread as far if the local people had been able to do something to stop it. The problem is that there is no fire fighting equipment anywhere in the town. This will now be provided on my orders.

In addition, sir, I was wondering whether you might allow us to form a fire brigade with just 150 members? I will make sure that only real fire fighters are allowed to join. It will be easy to keep a watchful eye on such a small number.

I look forward to your reply.

Yours

G. Plinius

Pliny

Gaius Plinius
Governor's HQ
Nicomedia
The province of Bithynia

Trajan
Imperial Palace
Rome

c. July AD 111

Dear Pliny

Thank you for the letter in which you ask permission to set up a fire brigade in Nicomedia. Unfortunately, I am unable to grant your request.

You must remember that it is organisations like the one you ask for which have been responsible for the trouble in your province. They have been a particular nuisance in towns. You see, if people get together in a group, they soon start organising rebellions against Roman rule - and we can't have that.

It would be better for you to provide the equipment for dealing with fires and to instruct local people to make use of it, should a fire break out. They can always call on bystanders to help if they are needed.

I hope all is well.

Yours

Traianus

The Emperor Trajan

The Governors

All Governors were Senators and many had been Consuls. They were in charge of their province and had to deal with any problems that arose there.

This page explains what a Governor did and the sort of problems that the Governor would be expected to solve.

Source B   Provincial government

Governor and his staff

Tax collectors

Army

Town councils

Ordinary people

Septimus Severus, Governor of Sicily in AD 188. He later became Emperor.

Source D   Governor's duties

1. Keeping the peace
2. Making sure that taxes are collected
3. Settling disputes
4. Acting as a judge in court
5. Controlling town councils

Source A   Defending the province

I arrived in my province on the 30th July after a slight delay due to the weather and have spent the last two months with the army.

As you know, there is danger of an invasion from Parthia. I have put my troops on full alert. Unfortunately, I discovered on my arrival that there were not enough troops to cope with a full-scale invasion. I beg you as a matter of urgency to send out reinforcements.

Letter from Cicero, Governor of Cilicia, to the Senate, October 51 BC

Source C   Controlling town councils

My first move was to examine the town council's accounts. As you might imagine, I soon found that some councillors had been on the fiddle. They were called into my office and ordered to pay back what they had taken. I could have been harder with them but it worked.

Letter from Cicero, Governor of Cilicia, to his friend Atticus, 50 BC

Activities

1. 'The Governor made all the important decisions.' Explain why using Sources B and D.

2. Place the Governor's duties (Source D) in order of importance and explain why you have chosen this order.

3. What do Sources A and C tell us about a Governor's job?

4. Look at the map on page 34. Why do you think Governors were put in charge of provinces rather than the Emperor ruling directly from Rome?

Taxes

Once an area had been made into a province the people who lived there had to pay taxes to the government in Rome.

Rome argued that taxes were necessary to pay for bringing peace to the provinces. Armies were very expensive. At the same time, Rome did do well out of it. The more provinces there were, the more money would be received from taxes.

The sources on this page look at Rome's system of taxation.

Source A

Rome has brought peace to the provinces. Taxes pay for the peace because they pay for the army. People living in the provinces, therefore, should not complain about paying taxes.

Cicero, letter to his brother, 51 BC

Source B

Rome cannot afford to lose provinces because the people living there pay so much in taxes.

Cicero, letter to the Senate, 51 BC

Source C   Zarai, Africa, AD 202

List of customs tax payable when goods pass through this customs station

Type of goods	Price
Slaves	1½ denarii
Animals:	
Horse, mare	1½ denarii
Sheep, goat	1 sesterce
Cattle for market	duty free
Imported cloth/hides:	
Purple cloak	1 denarius
Sheepskin	½ sesterce
Miscellaneous:	
Glue, per 100 pounds	½ sesterce
Wine, per amphora	1 sesterce
Garum (fish sauce)	1 sesterce

Did you know?

- From 167 BC people who lived in Rome and Italy did not have to pay certain taxes. The money from the provinces paid their share.

- After 123 BC the unemployed in Rome were allowed to buy corn at a reduced price (they made bread or porridge with it). Taxes from the provinces paid for this 'corn dole'.

Activities

1. Using the evidence on this page explain who paid taxes and what the taxes were used for. Was it a fair system?

2. Suppose that a farmer went to market every week and had to pass through the customs station at Zarai (Source C). If that farmer carried an average of:

   2 slaves
   5 animals (2 horses, 2 sheep, 1 cow)
   1 purple cloak
   2 sheepskins
   6 miscellaneous articles (2 of each)

   how much would have to be paid to the government each year?

   Give your answer in sesterces, denarii and aurei.

   4 sesterces = 1 denarius
   25 denarii   = 1 aureus

Boudicca's rebellion

What did people in the provinces feel about Roman rule? If we look at the growth of the Empire, we can see a pattern. When the Romans first invaded new lands, the local people did not like their new rulers. They hated paying taxes and felt they had lost their freedom. Often they rebelled and tried to drive the Romans out. If they did rebel, the Roman army was called in. Often large numbers of locals were killed. Afterwards there was little trouble.

Rebels left no written records, so our information about them comes from Roman sources. This is a problem because the Romans did not always understand the rebels' point of view.

On these pages, we look at a rebellion led by a Briton called Boudicca. Boudicca was Queen of the Iceni tribe who lived in East Anglia. The rebellion took place in AD 60, seventeen years after Britain was invaded.

Source A

The British leader Boudicca persuading her people to rebel:

Listen to me. You know the difference between freedom and slavery. Before the Romans came, we were free. Now we are slaves. When the Romans invaded us they robbed us of our riches. Now they continue to rob us by making us pay taxes. Every year we work on our land – and for what? So that they can take away all that we earn? I would rather die in battle than have to pay taxes. But why do I mention death? Even death isn't free any more. We even have to pay the Romans before we can bury our dead! They look down on us and trample us underfoot. All Romans care about is making money out of us.

Dio Cassius, c. AD 210

Source B   Boudicca's rebellion AD 60-61

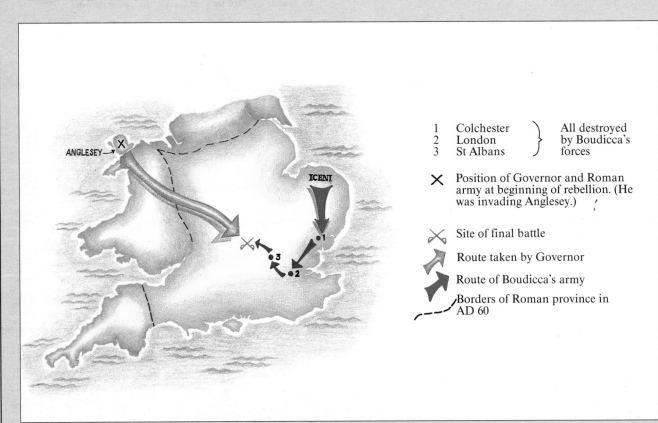

1	Colchester	All destroyed
2	London	by Boudicca's
3	St Albans	forces

✕ Position of Governor and Roman army at beginning of rebellion. (He was invading Anglesey.)

⚔ Site of final battle

➪ Route taken by Governor

➪ Route of Boudicca's army

- - - Borders of Roman province in AD 60

Source C

The Governor of Britain gave the signal for battle and the Romans threw their spears at the Britons. Then they charged at them. The Britons began to panic and tried to run away. But their wagons blocked them in. They were trapped. The Romans won a glorious victory. When Boudicca saw what had happened, she poisoned herself.

Tacitus' description of the final battle (written c. AD 120)

Source E

Boudicca's rebellion failed and was followed by many years of peace. But the price of peace was high. 80 000 people had been killed - a huge number (if correct). This table shows approximate figures only.

Population of the whole of Britain in AD 60	5 million
Population of the part of Britain ruled by the Romans in AD 60	2 million
Number killed in rebellion	80 000

Source D

A modern statue of the British leader Boudicca

Activities

1. Using the information on these pages, explain:
   a) why the Britons rebelled in AD 60;
   b) what happened during the rebellion.

2. Why do you think that there were many years of peace after Boudicca's rebellion?

Checklist

- The Roman Empire was too large to be governed entirely from the centre. The answer was provincial government.

- The main jobs of a Governor were to keep the peace, collect taxes, deal with problems and to take charge of the army in his province.

- Taxes benefited Rome itself but were unpopular in the provinces.

- Rebellions usually occurred shortly after an area became a province. People objected to paying taxes and felt they had lost their freedom. Boudicca's rebellion is a good example of this.

A hamburger restaurant in London...

... is very much like a hamburger restaurant in Moscow.

A Roman lamp from Syria...

... is very much like a Roman lamp from Britain.

Themes

Travel to New York, Moscow, Paris and London today and you will find shops which sell the same hamburgers, cinemas which show the same films, people wearing the same types of clothes.

If you travelled to any province in the Roman Empire in AD 150, you would have found similar buildings, shops which sold the same Roman lamps, bath houses with the same hot and cold rooms, people wearing togas.

The Romans ruled their Empire for many years. As time went on, people in the provinces got used to Roman rule and to the Roman way of life. Rebellions – like the one described in the previous chapter – became a thing of the past. People in the provinces began to admire and copy the Romans.

This slow process of change in the provinces is called Romanisation. This chapter looks at what happened when a province became Romanised.

Focus Activities

The interview on the Focus page has been put together from information in Tacitus' biography of his father-in-law, Agricola. Tacitus is one of the few Roman writers who discusses Romanisation. Use the interview to answer the following questions.

1. a) What does 'Romanisation' mean?
    b) How did Agricola encourage Romanisation?
2. What is Agricola's attitude towards people from the provinces? Does he think of them as equals? How do you know?
3. Why do you think Agricola wanted the British to become Romanised?

Interview between the historian, Tacitus, and his father-in-law, Agricola, Governor of Britain

Tacitus   Agricola, I believe that you have just returned from the province of Britain?

Agricola   That's right.

Tacitus   Could you tell me a little bit about what you found there?

Agricola   Yes, well as you know, it has only been forty years since we invaded Britain. Since then, although the British have begun to make a bit of progress, I am afraid to say that, on the whole, they are a pretty backward, uncivilised bunch.

Tacitus   Uncivilised in what way?

Agricola   The problem, as I see it, is that they have never lived in towns and so they don't understand the finer things in life. You see, before we invaded, they lived in villages which were controlled by local chieftains. As you can imagine, these chieftains were always arguing with each other and spent most of their time fighting wars. Of course, we've put a stop to all that and the next stage is to get them to live like Romans.

Tacitus   What steps have you taken to make sure that this happens?

Agricola   I must say that the Romans have never *forced* anyone to follow their way of life. What we do is lead by example and give a little push where necessary. The way we look at it, the most important people are the local leaders. They're the people who have the power and the money and so we approach them first.

Tacitus   And how do you get these leaders on our side?

Agricola   In two ways. First, we get them together and have a chat explaining what we can offer them. You know the sort of thing – 'Look here chaps, you're Romans now and and we're relying on you to behave like Romans. It's up to you. Get yourselves a Roman education and you'll soon see that the Roman way of life is for you.' Before you know it, the local leaders all want to be more Roman than you or I.

Tacitus   And the second way.

Agricola   As I've said, we lead by example. Now there are four legions in Britain. The soldiers come from all over the Empire. What we do is to get the older soldiers to set up Roman towns in the province. The soldiers live there and the locals see what's what. These are 'model' towns for the locals to copy.

Tacitus   So, what progress has been made?

Agricola   You must understand that things don't change overnight. Each province is different and so long as there are no wars, then we will not interfere. Give it a couple of hundred years and I am sure that Britain really will be a part of the Roman Empire.

'Model' towns

The Roman government did not force people to copy the Roman way of life, but it did help them. For example, in Britain there were no towns before the Romans invaded. But soon after the invasion, 'model' towns were built for the Britons to copy. These 'model' towns are the first signs of Romanisation.

'Model' towns were often based on the plan of a Roman fort. Sources A and B show this. Forts were built by soldiers and it was soldiers who built most of the 'model' towns.

'Model' towns contained Roman-style buildings. Sources C and D show this.

Source A

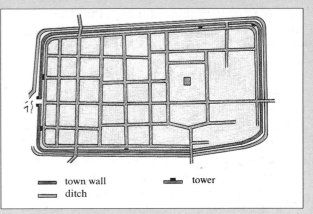

- — town wall
- — ditch
- — tower

Street plan of the 'model' Roman town at Colchester

Source C

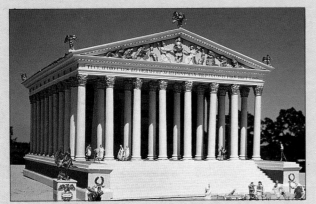

Reconstruction of the temple at Colchester

Source B

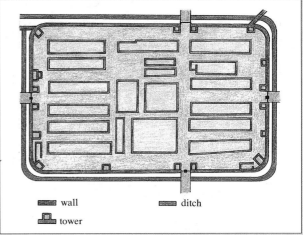

- — wall
- — ditch
- — tower

Plan of Housesteads fort, Hadrian's wall – a typical example of a Roman fort

Source D

The Maison Carré temple at Nimes in France is typical of temples found all over the Empire.

Activities

1. What do we mean by the term 'model' town?

2. Look at Sources A and B. Note any evidence which suggests that Colchester was based on a Roman fort.

3. Look at Sources C and D. Note any evidence which suggests that the temple at Colchester was based on a standard pattern found throughout the Empire.

The model towns were built so that the Britons could copy them. If they did copy them, then this would be a sign that the British were becoming Romanised. It would show that they were taking on the Romans' way of life.

As time went on, the Britons did build many towns. For example, Silchester (Source E) and Caerwent (Source G) were built by Britons. Silchester has a similar plan to other Roman towns. If you compare it with the plan of Pompeii in Italy (Source F) you will see many similarities. In fact Silchester had similar facilities to those found in towns throughout the Roman Empire.

Caerwent in Wales contains buildings that may have been designed by Roman army architects or copied from a Roman fort.

Source E   Silchester

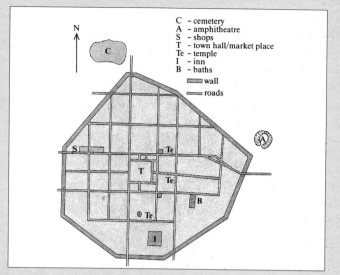

C – cemetery
A – amphitheatre
S – shops
T – town hall/market place
Te – temple
I – inn
B – baths

wall
roads

Plan of the remains of the Roman town at Silchester

Source G

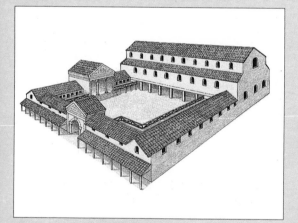

The market place at Caerwent in Wales

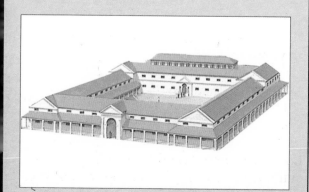

The headquarters building of a Roman fort

Source F   Pompeii

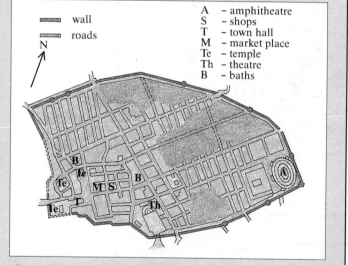

wall
roads
N

A – amphitheatre
S – shops
T – town hall
M – market place
Te – temple
Th – theatre
B – baths

Plan of the remains of the Roman town at Pompeii

Activities

1. a) Make a list of the similarities between Pompeii and Silchester (Sources E and F).
    b) How do these similarities show us that the Britons were becoming Romanised?

2. Using the evidence on both these pages, explain why the Roman army was important in the process of Romanisation.

Trade and Romanisation

It was not just the army which helped Romanisation to happen. As soon as there was peace in a new province, traders came from other provinces to sell their goods. Some came from lands far away from Britain – like Syria or Egypt. Others came from just across the Channel.

These traders brought new goods and ideas to the province. Some even ended up staying there for many years.

The result was that the population of the new province became more and more mixed with people from other provinces. People's way of life changed because they used the new goods and heard about the new ideas. They became Romanised, with the result that a person who travelled around the Empire would feel at home in Italy, Britain, Syria or any other province.

Source B   Military decorations

Medals given to soldiers for bravery

Source C

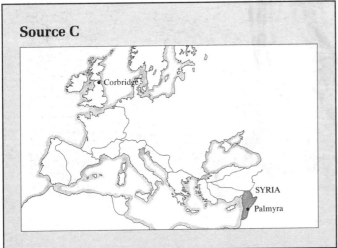

Source A   Tombstone

The inscription reads, 'Regina a free woman and wife of Barates, a man from Palmyra. A member of the Catuvellaunian tribe, she died aged 30.'

The sources on this page all concern a man called Barates. He is mentioned on the tombstone (Source A). He was a trader from Syria who had travelled to Britain (Source C). He sold military decorations (Source B). In Britain, Barates met a British woman called Regina and they married. They lived at Corbridge, just south of Hadrian's wall.

Activities

Using the evidence on this page explain:

a) why Hadrian's wall was a good place for Barates to visit;

b) what the story of Barates' life tells us about the process of Romanisation.

Romanisation was only possible if people and goods could move easily from one part of the Empire to another. The ancient world was a world without cars, trains or aeroplanes. Travel was therefore slower. It was more difficult and much more expensive to transport goods over a long distance.

But people living in the Roman Empire had benefits. There was peace which meant people could travel without fear. Also, there were plenty of towns. The growth of these towns encouraged trade and trade brought new goods and new ideas to people.

Barates was one of many traders to travel around the Empire. We know this because archaeologists have found many pieces of evidence about Roman trade. This page examines some of that evidence.

Amphorae

Today people usually transport liquid goods in glass or plastic bottles. In Roman times, glass was very expensive and plastic had not been invented.

Roman traders used amphorae (Source E) to carry liquid goods. Amphorae were usually made out of pottery. They were a special shape so that they could be sealed and stacked easily.

Source D   Samian ware pottery

These pots were made in Gaul. They were found in Britain. Later, similar pots were made by British potters.

Activities

1. Look at Source D. What does it tell us about the process of Romanisation?

2. Draw an outline of one of the amphorae in Source E and explain why it was designed like this. How would amphorae have been stacked? Draw your answer.

Source E

Underwater photograph showing amphorae in a shipwreck

Travel and transport

There were two types of transport in the ancient world – transport by water and transport by land. This page will look at transport by water, the facing page will look at transport by land.

Ships and river boats

The cheapest way to carry goods over long distances was by water. The Romans carried goods across the seas in ships and along rivers in boats. It was about ten times cheaper to carry a load by sea than it was by road. By river, it was about five times cheaper.

The ship in Source A could carry about 150 tonnes. Ships were sometimes larger than this. One Roman writer mentions a ship that could carry 1200 tonnes. But ships of that size were unusual. For one thing, if a big ship sank, more cargo would be lost. Roman ships often sank – many have been found on the bottom of the Mediterranean.

Reconstruction of a Roman ship

Did you know?

- Many Roman towns were built on the coast or by a river. The River Tiber flows through Rome. London became an important town in Roman times because it was on the River Thames.

- Roman ships rarely travelled out of sight of land. They usually sailed between the beginning of March and the end of October. Sailing was too risky at other times.

- Roman ships were powered by oars and one or two sails. They were steered by long oars near the back of the ship.

Source B

Two merchant ships – a Roman carving

Roads

Most Roman roads were built by the army so that soldiers could march quickly to a trouble spot. Once built, they were also used for travel and trade.

The standard of road building was very high. Some Roman roads can still be seen today (Source C). Many were being used in the nineteenth century. Modern roads often follow the route of old Roman roads. Source D shows how army road builders used different methods of construction in different situations.

Despite good roads, travel by road was still very slow. An ox and cart would probably travel no more than ten miles in a day. Road transport was also very expensive. A shipload of grain could travel from one end of the Mediterranean to the other (about 2500 miles) for the same price that it would cost to transport it 75 miles by land.

Source C

Via Appia Antica, Rome – a Roman road as it is today

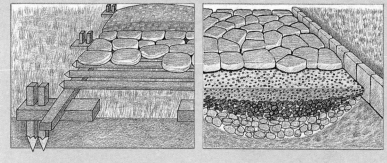

Source D   Methods of constructing roads

on wet ground   on dry ground

Activities

1. a) Compare the ships shown in Sources A and B. In what ways are they similar?
    b) How do archaeologists know that Roman ships looked like the one pictured in Source A?

2. Explain why transport by water was cheaper than transport by land.

3. Look at Source D.
    a) Describe each of the methods of road building.
    b) Explain why both methods were used.

4. How did improvements in travel and transport help the process of Romanisation?

Checklist

- People who lived in the provinces gradually began to copy the Roman way of life. This process is called Romanisation.

- It was mainly the army and traders who introduced people to the Roman way of life.

- People were able to travel all round the Roman Empire. This made it possible to exchange goods and ideas. Compared with today, travel was slow and transport expensive.

Labels on the drawing:
- cremation cemetery c.AD 50–AD 200
- sheep barn
- grain store
- shed
- pig sty
- servants' and farm labourers' quarters
- building with raised floor for dry storage
- soak-away
- drain
- wells
- great barn
- inhumation graves with stone sarcophagi 4th century AD
- privy
- villa
- storehouse
- stable
- cattle byre
- villa garden
- orchard
- orchard
- gravelled path
- perimeter wall

Drawing of a villa

Themes

In the Roman world, 75% of people worked on farms. In Britain today, less than 2% of people do so.

Rich people owned large farms called villas – like the one above. These farms were either run by the owner's slaves or the land was divided up and hired out to people who paid rent to the owner.

Poorer farmers usually grew only just enough food to feed their family and pay their taxes. Often life was very hard for them.

The 25% of people who were not farmers did many jobs. Most owned at least one slave. Some had many slaves working for them.

The Focus page looks at a small bakery business somewhere in the province of Africa. The owner has several slaves working for him.

Focus Activities

Read the story on the Focus page. The bakery is up for sale. You are an estate agent who visits the bakery before it is sold.

1. Write a report outlining what is for sale. Comment on the condition of the buildings, the animals and the workers.

2. Write a short speech to a possible buyer in which you:
   a) explain the advantages of running a mill and bakery in this way;
   b) try to persuade the buyer that it is a good buy.

3. Make a list of the problems that a baker might have had in the ancient world but would not have now.

A bakery and mill house

I met the baker at the local market where he had just bought a new mule. He had loaded it with a huge sack of corn and was preparing to make the long walk home. We began chatting and he invited me to come and see his place of work. 'It's a profitable little business,' he said, 'I'm sure you'll be impressed. I'm not just a baker, you know. I've got a mill house there too. I buy the corn, grind it into flour and then make it into bread.'

When we arrived, he began to show me around. I didn't think much of what I saw. The mill house was a huge dark room which contained several millstones, each one turned by a mule. The mule was blindfolded and harnessed to a large wooden pole which was attached to the millstone. It was forced to walk round and round in circles turning the millstone as it did so. If the poor beast stopped it was beaten until it started again. The baker told me proudly that the millstones never stood still. 'They are grinding out flour all day and all night too,' he boasted. No wonder the mules looked as if they were at death's door. The animals were

exhausted. If you looked closely in the dim light, you could see that their necks were covered in running sores where they had been beaten and their chests were rubbed raw from the harnesses.

And then there were the slaves who worked there. They were in no better condition than the mules. Most were dressed in rags. Their backs were covered in scars from the floggings they had been given. They had letters branded on their foreheads. They had irons on their legs. All of them had yellow complexions. Their eyelids were black with the smoke from the bread ovens and their eyes were so bleary and inflamed that they could hardly see out of them. They were caked from head to foot in a fine layer of dirty flour.

Each slave had a different job. Some made sure that the mules kept walking. Some stoked the fire and looked after the bread ovens. Some made the dough and kneaded the bread. Everyone worked in silence in this stuffy workshop. The sight of all this made me think how lucky I was not to work there.

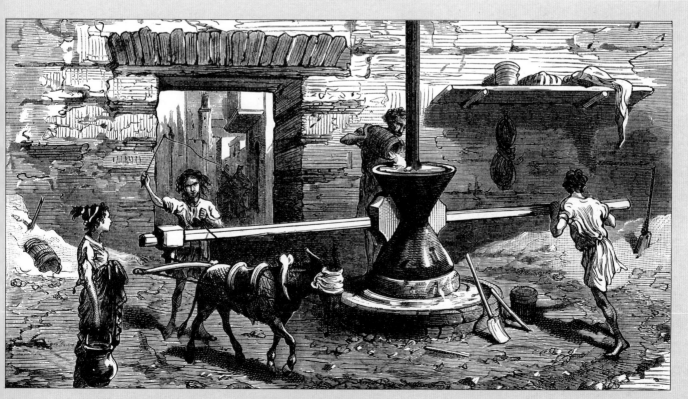

Roman corn mill – an engraving from the nineteenth century

Roman agriculture

The Roman invasion of Britain brought many changes in agriculture. New farms – villas – grew up (Source A) and stronger and better tools were made (Source B). Forests were cut down and new crops were grown (for example, grapes were grown in East Anglia for the first time).

A villa was not just a farmhouse. It was a centre of industry. Apart from several types of farming – growing crops for food, trees for timber and rearing animals – there were crafts like pottery and metalwork, and mining for coal and metals. The villas provided most of the food for people who lived in towns. Most villas were therefore near a town or a road.

Although Roman agriculture was efficient for its day, it was not as productive as modern farming. Fewer crops were produced from an acre of land and, without scientific breeding, animals produced less meat.

After the Roman conquest two things encouraged farmers to produce more.

- They now had taxes to pay.

- With more and more people living in towns they had a growing market to sell to.

Activities

1. Why were most villas clustered around towns (Source A)?

2. Some parts of Britain did not have villas (Source A). What does that tell us about the process of Romanisation?

3. What agricultural jobs were done by the tools in Source B?

4. Why did Roman farming employ more people than modern farming? Why was Roman farming less efficient?

Source A   Villas, towns and roads

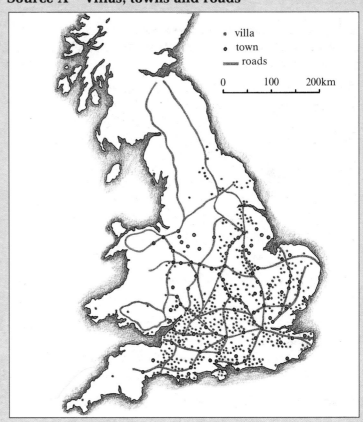

- villa
- town
- roads

0   100   200km

Source B

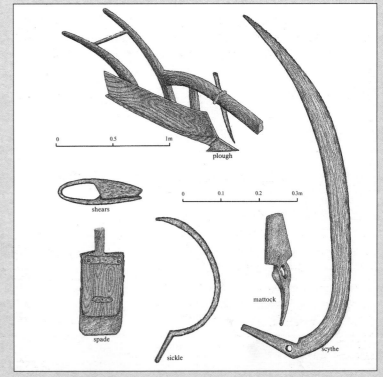

plough

shears

spade

sickle

mattock

scythe

0   0.5   1m

0   0.1   0.2   0.3m

Farming implements from Roman Britain

Slave labour

A slave is a person who is owned by another person in much the same way as a cow or a sheep is owned by a farmer.

In the ancient world slavery was normal. When a battle was fought captives were sold into slavery and from then on they had no rights. The children of slaves automatically became slaves themselves.

On the Focus page the baker does not treat his slaves very well. However, not all slaves were treated so badly. Some were better off than poor free people. Many slaves were allowed to buy their freedom. Their sons then became Roman citizens.

Source A

A slave being punished in a pillory

Source C

Cato bought many slaves who were captives taken in war. When at home a slave had to be either at work or asleep. After dinner, he would whip those slaves who had not prepared or served the food properly.

Plutarch, c. AD 120 (Cato lived in the 2nd century BC.)

Source D

Crassus was incredibly rich but none of his property compared with the value of his slaves. He had a huge number and variety – secretaries, readers, silversmiths and waiters to name but a few. He himself took charge of their training.

Plutarch, c. AD 120 (Crassus lived in the 1st century BC.)

Source B

A wealthy woman with four slaves

Source E

Sensible and well educated people should live on good terms with their slaves. If they hate us, it is our own fault for mistreating them. Remember that your slave was born, breathes, lives and dies just like you do. You should treat those below you as you would like to be treated by those above you.

Seneca, c. AD 55

Activities

1. Using the sources on this page, make a list of the different jobs done by slaves.

2. If you were a slave would you rather have Cato (Source C) or Seneca (Source E) as a master? Explain why.

3. Look at Sources A and C. How would people feel about these punishments in Britain today? Explain your answer.

4. What is happening in Source B? How do we know that the woman was wealthy?

Romans at work

Written evidence from Roman historians tells us a great deal about the lives of rich people. However, it says little about ordinary people. To find out about their lives and work we must turn to other types of evidence.

Tombstones are an important source of evidence. They tell us how long people lived and what they did. Apart from the very poor, most people could afford a tombstone.

Stone carvings are another important source of evidence. They sometimes give detailed pictures of everyday life.

The sources on these two pages tell us things about ordinary people which are not mentioned by Roman historians.

Activities

1. Make a table which shows the name, age, sex, status (slave or free) and occupation of the people on the tombstones (Source A).

Name	Age	Sex	Status	Job
Julia	45	Female	Free	Doctor

2. Most people died younger than would be expected today. Why do you think this was?

Source A

An artist's impression of a Roman cemetery. All the inscriptions have been taken from actual Roman tombstones.

Source B

Source C

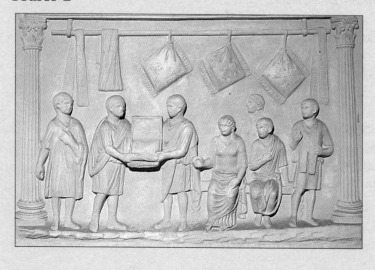

Source D

Source E

Activities

3. a) Why didn't ordinary people leave written records?
    b) Why do Roman historians have so little to say about ordinary people?

4. Explain what the people are doing in each of these carvings (Sources B–E).

5. List the tools and materials needed for one of the jobs shown in Sources B–E and say who would provide them. (For example, a fishmonger would need a shop, fish, knives, scales, plates and shelves which would have been provided by builders, fish merchants, metal workers, potters and carpenters.)

6. If you know someone who does one of these jobs today, show them the picture and ask:

    a) What are the people doing?
    b) What items are shown?
    c) How much have things changed since Roman times?

    Make notes on the answers and report back to the class.

Roman technology

Some historians believe that Roman technology was simple and primitive and that the Romans did not make new discoveries because they did not need them – they had slaves to do the work.

It is true that there were plenty of slaves and poor people to do the donkey work. But if there was a problem that needed a technological solution, the Romans often found a way of solving it. On these two pages there are examples of Roman technology. Some of these inventions were forgotten and not reinvented until many centuries later.

One reason that such inventions were rare is that they were local solutions to local problems. Ideas spread slowly in the ancient world.

On the Focus page the baker uses mules and slaves to grind his corn. On this page water power is used to grind corn at the mill in Gaul. Although today we may think that the water mill is better, the Romans were happy with both ways.

Source A   The Barbegal water mill

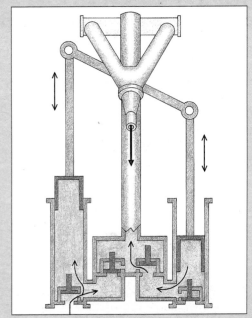

The Barbegal
water mill
1 principal
   doorway
2 loading area
   for carts and wagons
3 concrete platform
   for drying grain
4 central passageway with
   access to milling chambers
5 milling chamber
6 aqueduct feeding triangular
   reservoir
7 mill race
8 overshoot water wheel c. 2.2m
   diameter
9 wooden spout with panels which can
   be raised
10 wooden gearing mechanism
11 millstone 0.9m diameter
12 wooden trough for collecting flour
13 stairway

Reconstruction of a water mill at Barbegal in Southern France. It was used for making flour.

Source C   Archimedes screw pump

Used for draining water out of mines

Source B   Force pump

For pumping water out of boats or mines

Source D   A hypocaust

A mosaic floor laid over pillars of stone

The hypocaust system used hot air to heat houses and baths.

Source E   Aqueduct

The Pont du Gard aqueduct in France. Aqueducts were used to carry drinking water to towns.

Activities

1. The control of water was very important in the Roman Empire. Use Sources A, B, C and E to explain why.

2. Do you think Roman technology was 'simple and primitive'? Give reasons for your answer.

3. You have been travelling round the Roman Empire and discovered one of the inventions shown in Sources A to E. You return home and try to persuade your local town council to use the invention.

   Explain how it worked and why it would be useful. Draw diagrams and/or make models to help the councillors understand what you are talking about.

The theatre at Merida, North Africa

Model of an amphitheatre – the Colosseum, Rome

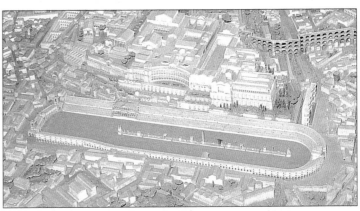

Model of Circus Maximus in Rome

Themes

Today people usually work for five days and take the weekend off. The Romans did not have weekends but they did have rest days and even rest weeks. These rest days were taken in order to celebrate a religious festival. At the time of Caesar's death almost a third of the year was filled with religious festivals.

To celebrate some of these festivals, public games were put on. People were able to go to chariot races at the circus, gladiatorial fights at the amphitheatre or plays at the theatre.

This chapter looks at ways in which the Romans filled their leisure time.

Focus Activities

The facing page describes the two most popular spectator sports in the Roman world. As many as 100 000 spectators would crowd into the Colosseum to watch gladiators fighting, or go to the Circus Maximus to watch the chariot races.

1. Are there any modern sports similar to those watched by the Romans? If so, describe the similarities.

2. What are the main differences between Roman sports and sports in Britain today?

3. Do you think you would have enjoyed Roman sports? Give reasons for your answer.

SPORTS NEWS

Venusian gladiators look fighting fit

The sleepy town of Venusia, South Italy, should come to life tomorrow when a team of gladiators fight it out to the death. The team, trained by Salvius Capito, looked impressive in training today.

Watch out especially for Phileros, a Myrmillo who fights with a small shield and sword. He has won eleven crowns for bravery and is expected to put up a good fight against the more heavily armed Samnite fighters. A large crowd is expected at the games. The spectators will be dazzled by the gladiators' expert sword work and bravery. These lads will fight to the end, make no mistake.

The Venusian Team

Retiarius – fights with a net and trident with armour on forearms

Myrmillo – curved sword, small shield, helmet and light armour

Samnite – straight sword, large shield, heavily armoured

Consentius comes from behind to win on last lap

With four out of the seven laps gone, Consentius, ace jockey with the green team, had it all to do. His chariot was trailing in fourth place and it seemed he had no chance. Then, suddenly, it all changed. The leading chariot began to slow and had to drop out of the race. Consentius saw his opportunity and made his move.

The rider in front panicked and took the bend too wide. Consentius aimed for the gap. As the three leaders levelled, it became clear that the other two were going to sandwich Consentius and bump him out of the race. Consentius flicked his whip and cleverly steered out of the way. The other two chariots collided and crashed into the circus wall. Consentius was home and dry. It was a remarkable comeback.

FIXTURES

The Colosseum, Rome
10 am to sundown
THE SHOW YOU SIMPLY CANNOT AFFORD TO MISS
10 000 gladiators, 12 000 wild animals, mock sea battle, Christians thrown to the lions and much more . . . Open all week

Amphitheatre, Venusia
10 am to sundown
Venusia's gladiators fight it out (see above)

Circus Maximus, Rome
11 am
Chariot racing
Greens v Blues (4 horse races)
Whites v Reds (2 horse sprints)

A day at the races

Charioteers raced in teams – the Greens, Blues, Whites or Reds. Throughout the Empire, charioteers would race for one of these teams. Supporters were loyal to their favourite colour, just as people today are loyal to their favourite football team. In AD 390, supporters rioted after their favourite charioteer was put into prison!

Successful charioteers were the popular heroes of their day. Although many were born slaves, they could win their freedom and great wealth at the races.

Gambling was very popular in the Roman world. This was one reason for the popularity of chariot races. Spectators would place bets on their favourite chariots.

Source A

Stone carving of a charioteer

Source B

I beg you demon, whoever you are, from this hour, from this day, from this moment, torture the horses of the Greens and Whites. Kill them! Make sure that the charioteers Clarus and Felix crash! Leave no breath in them! And then, let the Red team win.

Curse written on a lead tablet found in Africa

Source C

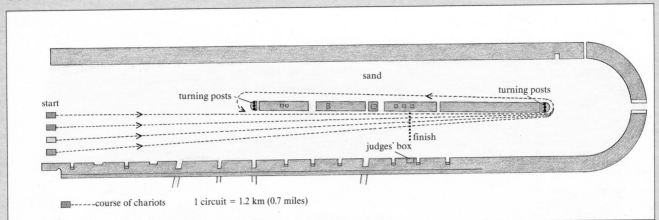

Plan of Circus Maximus showing the course of a chariot race

Source D

Source E   The world's top riders

World ranking	Name	Total no. of wins
1	Musclosus	3559
2	Scorpus	2048
3	Epaphroditus	1467
4	Diocles	1462

Source F   Gaius Diocles – Superstar

Full name:	Gaius Appuleius Diocles
Birthplace:	Lusitania, Spain
Age:	42 years, 7 months, 23 days
Born:	AD 104
Sport:	Chariot racing
Current team:	The Red Stable
Career:	Racing for 24 years
No. of races:	4257
No. of wins:	1462
No. of 2nd places:	861
No. of 3rd places:	576
Total winnings:	35 863 120 sesterces

Activities

1. Why do you think that the stone carving of a charioteer (Source A) was made?

2. Using Source C, explain how a chariot race was run.

3. Why do you think the curse (Source B) was written?

4. Your favourite team is riding against the Reds. Write a curse to be used against the Reds.

5. Write a short story about a chariot race using Sources C and D.

6. The tables in Sources E and F provide information about the charioteer Diocles.

   Write an article for a sports magazine which describes Diocles' career and explains why he was a sporting hero.

Bloodsports

Death has always fascinated people. Think of the last film you saw on TV or at the cinema. The chances are that someone was 'killed' in it. Of course, people do not really die in films. However, the fact that we watch these films for fun suggests that, even today, death can provide us with entertainment.

In ancient Rome, people really did die to provide entertainment for others. Crowds would flock to the local amphitheatre to watch trained gladiators fight to the death. Gladiators would fight each other or fight against wild animals, such as lions or panthers.

The crowd at the arena did not only watch gladiators fight. They would also see wild beasts fight each other or watch as hungry animals were let loose on unarmed criminals. On big occasions, the arena might be flooded with water and the crowd would be able to see a 'real' sea battle take place before their eyes. The one thing that all these events had in common was that they involved the killing of people or animals.

Source A   Programme of events

10 am	Procession around arena
10.30 am	Wild beast fighting
Midday	Execution of criminals
1 pm	Old gladiators fight with pretend weapons
2 pm	Serious fighting:
	1. Shadow fighting (to music)
	2. Fighters shout abuse
	3. Fight begins
	4. Loser asks the crowd to spare his life.

Source B   Gladiators

Mosaic showing a Samnite fighting a Retiarius with an umpire on the right

Source C

PLAZA DE TOROS DE LINARES

Jueves, dia 28 agosto de 1947

GRANDIOSA CORRIDA DE TOROS Tarde a las 4,45

Patrocinada por el Excmo. Ayuntamiento, con motivo de la

FERIA Y FIESTAS DE SAN AGUSTIN

Poster advertising a bullfight in Spain

Source D   The popularity of the games

There are only two things that people care about these days – bread and games.

Juvenal c. AD 100

What is it that young people talk about at home and at school? Actors, horses and gladiators!

Tacitus c. AD 120

Source E

Source F

COLOMBUS
SERENIANUS
LIES HERE.
HE WAS A
MYRMILLO WHO
FOUGHT 25 TIMES.
HE WAS BORN
IN GAUL.

Most, but not all, gladiators were slaves. Not all of them lived to fight as many times as Colombus.

Source G

I reached the arena at lunchtime expecting there to be a pause in the slaughter and hoping for some fun and relaxation. But not a bit of it. In the morning criminals had been thrown to the lions. Now they were forced to fight each other. When a man killed another he was then killed by the next. The crowd loved it. 'Kill him! Lash him! Burn him!', they shouted. 'Why does that one give in so easily? Give him a taste of the whip, that'll make him fight!' Not a moment is lost. The killing goes on and on all day long.

Seneca, c. AD 55

Activities

1. Why do you think people would choose to have the mosaic in Source B on their dining room floor?

2. Are people today really so different from Romans? Use Source C as part of your answer.

3. a) What did Seneca feel about the games (Source G)?
   b) Do you think most people thought the same? Explain your answer.

4. Colombus was a fairly successful gladiator (Source F). Briefly explain why.

5. You have just been on holiday in ancient Rome. Whilst you were there, you visited the arena and watched the games.

   Write a letter home explaining what you saw and what you thought of it. Describe the behaviour of the other spectators and explain why the games were so popular.

Roman games

Organised games in the amphitheatre or circus were not the only games that the Romans enjoyed. People spent much of their leisure time playing games amongst themselves. The bath house, for example, was not just popular because it was a place to relax and get clean. It was also a social club. People would exercise there and spend time chatting to their friends and playing games.

Dice games were especially popular – with Emperors and with ordinary people. People would gamble on a dice throw. We know that there were professional dice players and special names for certain throws – for example, three sixes was called a 'Venus'.

Roman board games have also been discovered. An example is shown in Source A.

Source A   Latrunculi

A Roman board game for 2 players. This game is best played on a draughtboard using draught pieces. Each team has 17 pieces. One piece is a 'dux' and should be specially marked. The object is to capture the opponent's pieces.

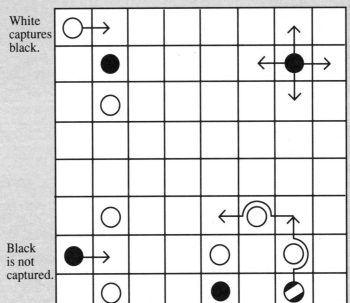

White captures black.

Possible moves that a piece can make.

A 'dux' can jump over one or more enemy pieces next to it. This shows a black 'dux' capturing a white piece. (It does not capture the pieces it jumps over.)

Black is not captured.

Stage 1
Place the pieces on the board one at a time. The 'dux' must be placed last. White goes first. You can place your pieces anywhere on the board. Place them carefully as their position will affect the game later.

Stage 2
When all the pieces have been placed, players make alternate moves. White goes first. A piece can move one square at a time in straight lines only (see example above). The 'dux' moves in the same way but it is allowed to jump over one or more enemy pieces next to it.

Capture
An enemy piece is captured when you trap it between two of your pieces. The captured piece is then removed and you have a second turn. If you move one of your own pieces between two enemy pieces, then it is not captured.

Ending the game
The game ends when one player has captured all of the enemy pieces. If 20 moves go without a capture, a 'blockade' is declared and the player with the most pieces left on the board wins.

The winner is hailed 'Imperator' (victorious general) by the loser and spectators.

Source B   Dice players

Source C

A game of knuckle-bones or jacks

Activities

1. Why do you think games like those in Sources A, B and C are still popular today?

2. Make your own board game based on a chariot race. All you need is a large piece of paper, some counters and one dice. The aim of the game is to get round the track as quickly as possible. Any number can play.

   Draw a board in the shape of the Circus Maximus (see page 58). Divide the track into 50 squares and number them. Choose 10 squares and colour them in. If you land on one of these squares, your horses go out of control and you have to throw a six before you can carry on. Choose another 5 squares and colour them in a different colour. If you land on one of these squares, your horses get extra energy and you can move on 3 spaces.

   Each counter is a chariot and starts from square number 1. You move by throwing the dice. Decide on the number of laps before you start. The winner is the first player to finish the race.

Checklist

- The Romans enjoyed watching and playing sport as much as people do today. The most popular sports were chariot racing and gladiatorial shows.

- People supported their favourite chariot team and placed bets on the races. Some charioteers became superstars.

- Gladiatorial combats were very gruesome. Today, most people would not approve of a 'sport' which involved the death of other people. Some Romans disagreed with killing for sport but most enjoyed watching the fights.

- The Romans also played games. These are similar to the sort of games that people play today.

10 FAMILY LIFE

Reconstruction of apartment blocks at Ostia, near Rome

Themes

The picture above shows a block of flats at the port of Ostia, a few miles from Rome. Roman families used to live in flats like these. This chapter looks at the everyday life of the Roman family.

- What did people eat?
- What special occasions did the family celebrate?
- What did Roman homes look like?

Roman historians tell us a lot about generals and politicians but not very much about everyday life. How then are we able to find out about it? This chapter will provide clues which should help to answer this question.

We begin with an invitation to dinner from a wealthy landowner, Gaius Pompeius Trimalchio. Trimalchio appears in a story written in the reign of the Emperor Nero.

Focus Activities

When rich Romans had a meal they did not sit at the table. They lay on their fronts on couches which were arranged in a square. The meal was set before them on tables brought in by slaves. Romans usually ate with their hands, though they might use a spoon.

1. You have been invited to a meal at Trimalchio's villa. Write a short account of the meal for a cookery programme on TV. Mention the food, how it was served, the entertainment and the conversation.

2. Why do you think that many wealthy Romans gave dinner parties like this?

3. What do you think slaves who served the food and provided the entertainment thought about such dinner parties?

MENU DE LA MAISON

Les hors d'oeuvres

Green and black olives
Stuffed dormice served in a honey and poppyseed dip
Sausages on a bed of damsons and pomegranates
Pastry peahen eggs with a baked blackbird fillet within

First course

Zodiac pie – a speciality

*A circular pie which is based on the twelve signs of the zodiac –
whatever your own star sign may be, our chef will have created something to your taste!*

Roast hare and crisp young pig with a rich wine sauce
Deep-sea fish swimming in a lake of gravy

This course is accompanied by 100 year old Falernian wine.

Main course

Wild Boar

Specially roasted for the occasion, this huge beast will be cooked and prepared in our own kitchens. Our chefs will decorate it with baskets of dry Egyptian and sweet Syrian dates and the boar will be surrounded by pastry piglets. And that's not all. Within its belly lurks a succulent surprise – live thrushes. Our slaves will be on hand to trap and cook them to your own special requirements.

Home-baked white bread and wine from Terracina will accompany this course.

Third course

Pork sculptured into the shape of a goose
Seasonal vegetables

Dessert

Honey cakes filled with liquid saffron
Pastry birds with raisin and nut stuffing

Throughout the meal, Trimalchio's trained slaves will entertain you. Singing, juggling and dancing are just three of the many acts for you to watch. We pride ourselves on our service and try to see to your every comfort. Make no mistake, this will be a meal to remember.

Food and drink

Only very rich Romans could afford the sorts of meals eaten by people like Trimalchio. Many people could not afford to eat meat very often and would only be able to buy food that was produced locally. Poor people lived mainly on coarse bread and a type of porridge made from barley and wheat.

The menu on the Focus page contains some unusual dishes. The Romans ate many creatures that people today would not want to eat. Some of these are pictured in Source A.

But how do we know what the Romans ate? There are two sorts of evidence. First, Roman authors sometimes mention food – though usually they write about the food that the rich ate. Perhaps our best source is the cookbook written by Apicius in the first century AD. Two of his recipes appear below (Sources B and C).

Second, there is archaeological evidence. By studying the remains found on Roman sites, archaeologists can work out what was eaten by the people who lived there. Source D shows the remains found in a typical Roman rubbish pit.

Source A

Creatures eaten by the Romans

Source C   Liquamen

This sauce was so popular that it was produced in factories and sold all round the Empire. It was used to flavour savoury dishes.

Ingredients

2 tablespoons of strong red wine
3 ounces of salt
3 anchovies (small fish with a strong flavour)
1 teaspoon of oregano (a herb)

Mix all the ingredients in a saucepan. Boil gently for 10 minutes. Cool and strain through muslin cloth. Store in a jar.

Source B   Rissoles

Ingredients

5 eggs	Honey
Breadcrumbs	Dash of pepper
Pinch of oregano	Brains of one pig
½ pint of liquamen	Pinch of lovage (a herb)
2 tablespoons of cooking wine	

Put the pepper, lovage, oregano, liquamen and cooked brains into a mixing bowl and pound it until all the lumps are broken up. Add the eggs and beat into a smooth paste. Cook over a slow fire and when ready take out and cut into pieces.

For the sauce

Take pepper, lovage, oregano, liquamen, honey and wine. Crush and then boil in a saucepan. Sprinkle in breadcrumbs to thicken the sauce. Pour over pieces of rissole.

Source D   A Roman rubbish pit

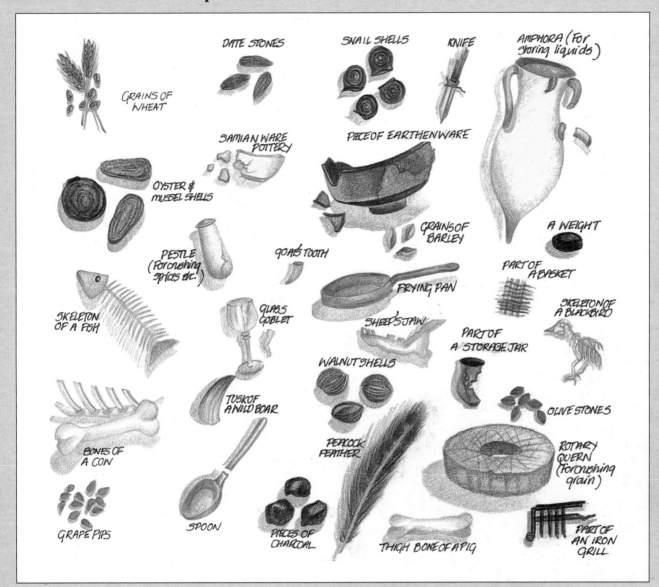

GRAINS OF WHEAT

DATE STONES

SNAIL SHELLS

KNIFE

AMPHORA (for storing liquids)

SAMIAN WARE POTTERY

PIECE OF EARTHENWARE

OYSTER & MUSSEL SHELLS

GRAINS OF BARLEY

A WEIGHT

PESTLE (for crushing spices etc.)

GOAT'S TOOTH

FRYING PAN

PART OF A BASKET

SKELETON OF A FISH

GLASS GOBLET

SHEEP'S JAW

SKELETON OF A BLACKBIRD

WALNUT SHELLS

PART OF A STORAGE JAR

TUSK OF A WILD BOAR

OLIVE STONES

BONES OF A COW

PEACOCK FEATHER

ROTARY QUERN (for crushing grain)

GRAPE PIPS

SPOON

PIECES OF CHARCOAL

THIGH BONE OF A PIG

PART OF AN IRON GRILL

Activities

1. Look at Source A. Would you eat any of these creatures? Briefly explain why or why not.

2. What do Sources B and C tell us about Roman tastes?

3. Study Source D.

a) Make a list of the different sorts of food eaten by the Romans who used this rubbish pit.

b) Do you think they had a healthy diet?

c) Would they have eaten any other foods?

d) What does Source D tell us about how the Romans prepared and cooked their food?

The household

A Roman household included not only the members of the family but also the household slaves. All but the very poorest families would have slaves living in their houses.

As with many families today, children would usually live with their parents until they were married. Source A shows a typical Roman household.

Source B shows the paterfamilias (the father of the family). He was the head of the household and had total control over family affairs. Everyone had to obey him.

Source A   A Roman household

The paterfamilias owned all the family's possessions – even those of his children who had grown up. No matter how old the children were, they remained under his control. The only exception was when a daughter married. She then had to obey her husband's paterfamilias.

The paterfamilias in Source B is telling a slave to count out the money which his grown-up son is allowed to spend on his own family.

Source C shows a Roman marriage. Marriages were often arranged by the parents – at least amongst richer families. Sometimes an arranged marriage was made for political reasons – for example, Pompey married Julia, Julius Caesar's

Source B   The paterfamilias

daughter, in 60 BC to strengthen the bond between the two men.

Women were allowed to marry at the age of twelve. They might be engaged before that. The Emperor Claudius' daughter Octavia was engaged when she was just one year old.

The marriage ceremony took place in the bride's family home. There would be a feast. Then everyone would go to the husband's house. When they arrived, the bride rubbed fat on the doorposts and hung wool from them. Her husband then carried her into the house in case she slipped – which would be a bad omen.

Source C   A marriage ceremony

Source D shows the day a baby is born. The child was placed on a table in the main room. The father then lifted it up to show that he accepted it as a member of the family. On the eighth or ninth day, the child was named at a special ceremony.

Many children died young (especially those from poor families). Sometimes unwanted children were abandoned at birth. This was not illegal. However, they were often rescued by people who were childless or by people who would later sell them as slaves.

Source D   The newborn child

Source E   A Roman classroom

Source E shows a Roman classroom. Rich children might be educated at home but most went to school in the local town. Girls and boys would go to school between the ages of six and eleven. They were usually taught by slaves and would learn little more than how to read, write and add up.

Source F shows a boy at a special ceremony. He is putting on a special white toga to show that he is now an adult and a Roman citizen. The ceremony usually took place on March 17th in the year in which the boy was fourteen. There was no ceremony for girls.

Source F   Growing up

Activities

1. The pictures (Sources A–E) from the 'family album' show important events in Roman family life. What important family events are included in photo albums today? Apart from the costumes, would the pictures on these two pages look out of place in a modern family album?

2. Make a list of the similarities and differences between Roman family life and family life today. Use the following headings, a) The power of the father, b) Marriage, c) Birth, d) Education, e) Becoming an adult.

3. Girls and women in Roman times were treated as second class citizens. How does the information above show this?

The typical house

Source A shows a plan of a typical Roman house. The drawing is based on several houses found at Pompeii in Italy. Most Roman houses had an atrium. This was the central room. It was a partly covered courtyard with a pool in the middle to catch the rainwater.

Source A   Plan of a Roman house

B = bedroom, T = toilet

Source B

The atrium in a Roman house at Pompeii

Most houses would have simple furniture. But rich people might decorate their rooms with expensive pieces. Cicero once paid one million sesterces for a special table.

The chair in Source C was made of bronze. Chairs with backs like this were special and expensive. Several have been found at Pompeii.

Source C is a wall painting. The Romans did not have wallpaper. Instead, artists were employed to paint scenes from everyday life or mythology.

Activities

1. Draw a plan of your house. How does it compare with the plan shown in Source A?

2. Why was an atrium suitable for Pompeii, in Italy, but less suitable in Britain?

3. What information does Source C provide? Why are wall paintings especially useful for today's historians?

4. The picture in Source C has been called 'a love scene' and 'a music lesson'. What does that tell us about the problems historians have in finding out about the past?

Source C

Man and woman sitting on a chair

As well as painting their walls, the Romans decorated their floors with mosaics. Mosaics were made out of small pieces of stone, glass and tiles called 'tesserae'. They were cemented together to make a picture. People would choose their design from pattern books provided by the mosaic cutter. Mosaics would often be found in dining rooms because they were nice to look at and easy to clean.

Source D

Mosaic cutter at work

Source E   Roman mosaic of a villa

Activities

5. Use Sources D and E to work out how mosaics were made. Explain each stage from the design idea to the finished product.

6. Make your own mosaic. You may like to base it on a picture from this book.

   a) Draw the outline of your design on a piece of white card.

   b) Use a ruler to divide the card into small squares.

   c) Make the pieces of the mosaic out of coloured paper, bottle tops, etc.

   d) Stick the mosaic pieces onto the card.

Checklist

- Most people had a simple diet. But the rich might eat huge feasts.

- Some recipes survive. But most information about food comes from archaeological sites.

- The head of the Roman family was the paterfamilias.

- Special ceremonies took place when a child was born, when a boy reached adulthood, and when a person got married.

- A typical Roman house would have an atrium. It might also be decorated with wall paintings and mosaics.

ROMAN RELIGION

Themes

The Romans did not believe in just one god as, for example, Christians do. They believed there were many gods.

These gods not only looked like people, they also behaved like people. In Roman myths, they fell in love, fought wars, went to parties and had arguments just like people do. The main difference was that gods were immortal – they lived forever.

This chapter looks at the following questions.

- How did Roman religion work?

- What happened when the Romans came across new gods in the provinces?

- What was it like to follow one of the new religions which became popular during the Principate?

Juno, goddess of marriage

Minerva, goddess of wisdom

Jupiter, King of the gods

Focus Activities

Every year on January 1st the new Consuls had to perform a sacrifice to Jupiter, King of the gods, to make sure that they had a successful year in office. You were in the crowd watching the sacrifice described on the Focus page. Write a short article for a magazine which explains:

a) what the Romans in the crowd felt as they watched the ceremony;

b) what people today might think about the sacrifice;

c) why the ceremony took place and what might happen if it did not.

The sacrifice

The time is 63 BC. The scene is ancient Rome. Somehow we must get the gods on our side. If we fail, the mighty Roman Empire will crumble and fall. To succeed we must give the gods what they want. Blood must flow.

The new Consuls, Cicero and Antonius, wearing purple bordered togas, walk slowly up the Sacred Road to the temple of Jupiter, King of all the gods. The crowd falls silent. The Consuls take their places in front of the temple, sitting on ivory chairs.

Two snow white bulls are led forward to the altar in front of the temple steps. The bulls' horns have been

A bull about to be sacrificed

decorated with ribbons and painted gold. Once the bulls are in place a flute player begins to play so that no ill-omened sounds will be heard. The Chief Priest comes forward. He washes his hands and chants a prayer. He begins to sprinkle flour over the bulls and raises two knives towards the heavens. His words are spoken in a slow dull tone. Every word is exact – if he makes a mistake the ceremony will have to start again.

At last he is ready. He makes a sign to his assistant who shouts, 'I am about to strike'. With one move the assistant lifts a huge hammer and crashes it down onto the head of the first bull. He lifts it again and stuns the second. The Priest hands the knives to the Consuls and they walk calmly over to the fallen animals. Each Consul grabs the head of a bull and lifts it first upwards and then downwards. In unison they seize a bull by the chin and slit its throat. As the blood flows attendants collect it in bowls and the Priest makes a prayer to Jupiter. Within seconds the Consuls have also slit open the bulls' stomachs. They stand waiting for the Priest. The Priest examines the innards of each bull and pulls out the liver. He inspects it carefully and says it is suitable. This is a good omen.

The bulls' innards are thrown onto the altar fire as an offering to Jupiter. As the smoke drifts towards heaven and the smell of burning meat reaches the crowd, the bulls are cut up into steaks which are piled onto huge plates. Now that Jupiter has his share, the Roman people can enjoy a feast.

Traditional religion

To the Romans the world was full of mysteries. Why was it that one year a farm would have a bumper crop and another year the crops would fail? Why was it that someone who was perfectly healthy would suddenly become ill? Why would some ships sail across the sea without a hitch whilst others would be caught in a storm and wrecked?

Nowadays we try to use science to explain these things. The Romans did not. If something appeared to happen by chance, they often thought that it was the work of the gods.

The search for omens

The Romans believed that the gods gave signs which told people whether or not they should do something. These signs are called omens. When an important decision had to be made Romans would look for omens. If the omens were good this meant that the gods liked the decision. Omens were usually found in nature. For example, if a group of birds flew across the sky from left to right during a sacrifice this might be seen as a good omen.

Source A

Priest feeding the sacred chickens

An animal's liver was very important in the search for omens. The shape, colouring and markings on a liver were used for finding out whether the gods were sending a good or a bad omen. Source B shows a bronze liver. It was probably used as a model to help priests to 'read' a liver. Source A shows the sacred chickens. If a priest wanted to find out whether the gods liked a decision, grain would be given to the chickens. The way in which the chickens ate the grain would show the priest whether or not the gods liked the decision.

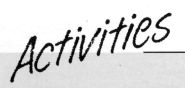

Many people today believe in superstitions. They think that certain things, such as a black cat crossing their path, show good or bad luck. In other words, they believe in omens.

1. Make a list of modern superstitions. Explain how they are supposed to affect people's behaviour.

2. Why do you think people believe in superstitions?

3. What are the similarities between Roman beliefs and modern superstitions?

4. Why were sacred chickens and bronze livers (Sources A and B) useful to Roman priests?

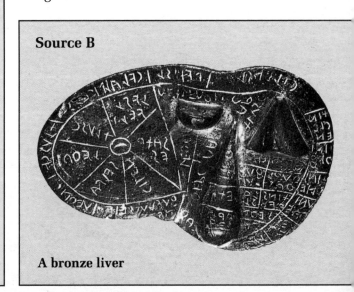

Source B

A bronze liver

Gaining the support of the gods

The Romans believed that success or failure depended on the support of the gods and that it was possible for people to win this support. They could do this by promising to give a god a gift. If people then had success, they would give the gift to the god.

A gift might be a sacrifice such as the one described on the Focus page. For example, a farmer might sacrifice a pig or a sheep in the hope of a good harvest. Or, a gift might be a special offering. Source C describes an offering of money to the god Jupiter made by a traveller who had returned home safely after a long journey.

Because there were so many gods, the Romans had to be careful to promise a gift to the right one. If people asked a god for something but did not get it, this would not make them think that the gods did not exist. Instead, they might think that they had made a promise to the wrong god, or they had not asked in the right way, or they had annoyed another god by mistake.

Source C

> To the divine Jupiter, I, Vassinus, made a vow before I left home on a journey. I promised to pay six denarii to the gods if they brought me home safely. Thanks to the gods I completed my journey unharmed. This inscription has been set up as proof that I have paid what I owed.

An offering made to Jupiter by a traveller after he returned home safely.

Inscription found at Stony Stratford, Britain

Source D

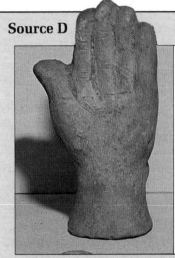

A pottery hand – someone with an injured hand had promised Aesculapius, the god of medicine, that a gift would be made if the hand got better. The pottery hand was placed in a temple as a gift.

Source E   The main gods

Name	Interest
Aesculapius	Medicine
Apollo	Music
Bacchus	Wine
Diana	Hunting
Jupiter	The whole world
Juno	Marriage
Mars	War & farming
Mercury	Trade & commerce
Minerva	Wisdom
Neptune	Sea
Pluto	Death
Venus	Love
Vulcan	Fire

Activities

1. Why did Vassinus (Source C) promise to pay 6 denarii? Why did he pay it only after he returned home?

2. Imagine you were a Roman who had fallen over and broken a leg. How would you explain what had happened and what would you do?

3. You are either a soldier, a sailor, a trader or a teacher. Explain which god would help you do your job well. How would you get that god's support?

Roman gods in the provinces

When the Romans invaded new lands, they found that the local people believed in gods that were new to them. Equally, the locals did not know of the Roman gods until they met the Romans. So, what happened when these different gods met?

Very often a god from the provinces was joined with a Roman god to make a new god. For example, Sulis was a British god and Minerva was Roman. At Roman Bath a new god Sulis Minerva was worshipped (Source B). Similarly, Antenociticus was a British god and Mars was Roman. At Benwell, near Newcastle-upon-Tyne, a new god Mars Antenociticus was worshipped.

The Romans worshipped these new gods in the same way as they worshipped their own. As time went on, local people copied Roman customs and worshipped the gods in Roman style. They built temples and made statues. Before the Roman invasion, there were no temples or statues of gods in Britain.

Statue of the Roman god Mars found at Lincoln and made by a local British artist

Source B

Bronze head of Sulis Minerva found at Bath

Source C

Altar dedicated to Mars Antenociticus found at Benwell, Newcastle-upon-Tyne

Although artists and builders learned from the Romans they did not just copy. They had their own style. Source D shows a Romano-British temple. Although it was similar to Roman temples, it had a different style. Compare it to the temples on page 42.

Compare it to the temples on page 42.

Source D

Romano-British temple at Caerwent

Source E

Claudius as a god. The eagle next to him is a special sign usually shown with Jupiter, King of the gods.

Human gods

The Romans thought that their gods looked like people. Every temple contained a statue of its god. The statues all looked like people.

Therefore, it is not surprising that the Romans believed that some people were god-like and became gods after their death. The first Roman to be worshipped as a god after his death was Julius Caesar. Augustus, the first Emperor, also became a god when he died in AD 14.

Many Emperors and their relatives (men and women) became gods after their death. Worship of them is known as the 'Imperial cult'. Like other gods they had temples and priests. Source E shows Claudius as a god. He became a god after he died in AD 54.

Activities

1. What did the Romans think about new gods? How do we know?

2. What effect did the Roman conquest have on religion in Britain (Sources A–D)?

3. Use Sources C and D to draw a plan of a Roman temple. What would you expect to find inside the temple?

4. Why do you think that some Emperors became gods after their death (Source E)?

5. Why do you think that it is difficult to find out about British religion in the years before the Roman conquest?

77

The cult of Mithras

From time to time new cults (special forms of worship of one particular god or group of gods) became popular in the Roman world. Often these cults came from outside the Empire. One was called 'Mithraism'. It became very popular in the second and third centuries AD.

Followers of Mithraism worshipped the Persian god Mithras. They held secret ceremonies in a small temple called a Mithraeum. Source A shows a Mithraeum which was found at Carrawburgh next to a fort on Hadrian's wall. Several of these temples have been found in Britain.

Although Mithraism was a secret cult, historians have been able to work out that:

- Mithraism was popular with soldiers (Source A).

- People who joined the cult had to undergo special tests (ordeals) and went to ceremonies in dark, incense-filled temples.

Mithraeum at Carrawburgh, next to Hadrian's wall

- Mithraism allowed worship of other gods as well, including the traditional Roman gods (Source B).

- According to legend Mithras slayed a bull and from the bull's blood all life was born (Source C).

Source B

The Roman god Mercury

The Egyptian god Serapis

Two objects found in the Mithraeum at London

Source C

Mithras slaying a bull

Did you know?

- Followers of Mithras celebrated their god's birthday which fell on December 25th. Later on, Christians took over this celebration and it became Christmas day.

- No women were allowed to go to Mithraic ceremonies.

- 7 was a magic number in Mithraism. There were seven grades of followers. To be promoted, a follower had to pass a test – for example, staying in a Mithraeum overnight without food or water.

- Different grades wore different costumes. Some of the grades were Lion, Raven, Bridegroom, Soldier and Father.

Activities

1. How do we know that Mithraism was popular with soldiers (Source A)?

2. Use the information on these pages to describe what it was like to be a member of this secret cult.

3. Describe the kind of evidence that a museum designer might need to make a reconstruction of a Mithraeum.

   a) What would the designer be certain about?

   b) What would have to be guesswork?

   c) How could the reconstruction be made attractive for visitors?

Checklist

- The Romans believed that the world was full of gods who played a part in human life. It was therefore important to gain their support.

- People looked for signs from the gods (omens) and promised them gifts to gain their support.

- Things we now explain by science were often explained by religion.

- The Roman gods were worshipped throughout the Empire. New gods from were accepted and often Roman gods.

- Secret cults such as Mithr became very popular. Beca secret it is difficult to find them.

80

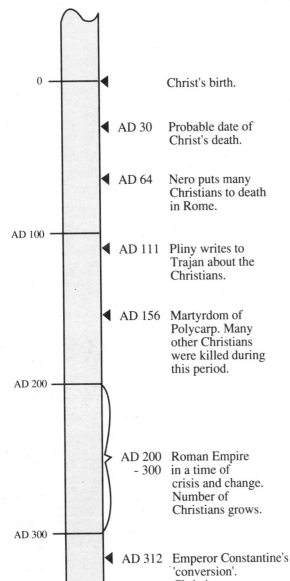

0	Christ's birth.
AD 30	Probable date of Christ's death.
AD 64	Nero puts many Christians to death in Rome.
AD 111	Pliny writes to Trajan about the Christians.
AD 156	Martyrdom of Polycarp. Many other Christians were killed during this period.
AD 200 - 300	Roman Empire in a time of crisis and change. Number of Christians grows.
AD 312	Emperor Constantine's 'conversion'. Christians are no longer persecuted.

Constantine

Themes

There are over 944 million Christians in the world today. But Christianity has not always been so popular.

Jesus Christ lived in the Roman province of Judaea. It was the Governor of Judaea, Pontius Pilate, who ordered him to be put to death. So, Christianity was a religion that began in the Roman world.

Christians believe that there is only one god. They must worship that god and no other. Early Christians refused to worship Roman gods. Because of this, they got into trouble. Many preferred to die rather than change their beliefs.

As Christianity became more popular, the Roman Empire fell into decline. From the third century AD, there was a crisis. This crisis would eventually result in the fall of the Roman Empire.

This chapter looks at Roman attitudes towards Christianity, and the decline of the Roman Empire.

Focus Activities

The Focus describes the martyrdom of Polycarp. Martyrs are people who die for their beliefs. Polycarp was one of the many Christians killed in the second and third centuries AD.

1. Do you think the Governor wanted to execute Polycarp? Explain your answer.

2. Why do you think the crowd wanted to kill him?

3. Why was Polycarp ready to die?

4. What does the author of the Focus think about Christians? Make a list of words and phrases which show this.

The martyrdom of Polycarp, AD 156

I saw them come to get him. He was an old man and a true believer in Christ. They arrested him and took him to the amphitheatre. On the way they kept trying to make him swear an oath to the Emperor. 'All you've got to do,' they said, 'is to swear that you will obey the Emperor and then make a sacrifice to the gods – it's easy'. At first he did not reply. Then all he said was, 'I will not do it'. It was then that they began to kick and beat him. It had no effect. He smiled and prayed for them under his breath.

At the amphitheatre, he was brought to the Governor. The Governor called for silence and this is what he said.

Governor	Is your name Polycarp?
Polycarp	It is.
Governor	Are you one of those who is called a Christian?
Polycarp	I am.
Governor	You are an old man. Save yourself. Change your mind. All you have to do is swear an oath to obey the Emperor and I will release you.
Polycarp	I have served Christ for 86 years and he has done me no wrong; how can I betray him now? Jesus is the King whom I serve.
Governor	Look, I have wild beasts. If you will not change your mind I will throw you to them.
Polycarp	Bring them in. They won't make me change my mind. We Christians know what is right and wrong and nothing you can do will make us stray from the path of good.
Governor	If the beasts do not scare you, then I'll have you burnt alive.
Polycarp	You threaten me with a fire that burns for an hour or so, but on the day of judgement

St Sebastian – a Christian martyr killed by the Romans

it is you who will burn in the fires of hell. Do what you wish.

At this the crowd went wild. 'Kill him,' they shouted, 'feed him to the wild beasts, burn him'. People began to collect sticks and logs and piled them up. Polycarp was pushed towards the pile and his tunic was ripped off. Men grabbed him and tied him to a stake. Someone got hold of a burning branch and set the pile alight. Polycarp stood there calmly. He smiled at his attackers and prayed for their souls. Then suddenly a great flame rose heavenwards and we all saw a dove fly up out of the fire. The soul of Polycarp had gone to heaven and he had taken his place at God's side with all the other saintly martyrs.

Early Christianity

The last chapter showed that the Romans often accepted new gods. But Christianity was different. Christians believed that there was only one god. Because of this they refused to worship the Roman gods. Many Christians also refused to swear an oath of loyalty to the Emperor.

Christianity spread from Judaea quickly. Although the exact date of Jesus' death is not known, historians agree that he died in the reign of the Emperor Tiberius (AD 14-37). Source D shows that there were Christians in Rome just 30 years after Jesus' death.

For 300 years it was illegal to be a Christian. Although the government did not go looking for Christians, if Christians were found, they would be executed unless they gave up their beliefs. This forced them to be secretive.

Source B   The Commandments

1. You shall worship no other gods except the one true God.
2. You shall not make any statues or other images of the one true God.

'The Book of Exodus' in the 'Old Testament'; chapter 20, verses 3-5

Source D

In AD 64, the Emperor Nero was becoming unpopular. He looked for someone to blame and chose people who belonged to a new religion called Christianity.

Nero arrested many of these Christians and put them to death. Most people agreed that they deserved to be punished for being Christians but so many were killed that people began to feel sorry for them.

Tacitus, c. AD 200

Source A

Emperor Trajan   Gaius Plinius
Imperial Palace   Governor's HQ
Rome   Bithynia

AD 111

Dear Sir

A new religion called Christianity is becoming very popular here.

If people are brought to me and accused of being Christians, I give them a test. I ask them if they are Christians. If they say 'yes', I threaten them with punishment and ask them again. If they keep saying 'yes', they are executed.

If they say 'no', I order them to repeat a prayer to our gods and to make a gift to a statue of you. Then I order them to curse Christ. Real Christians would refuse to do this.

I hope you agree that this is the best way to act.

Yours

G. Plinius

Pliny

Source C

Gaius Plinius   Emperor Trajan
Governor's HQ   Imperial Palace
Bithynia   Rome

AD 111

My dear Pliny

Thank you for your letter concerning the Christians.

You are quite right to do what you have done. However, do not go looking for Christians. Just deal with cases that are brought to you.

If they are guilty they must be punished. But if they are innocent and prove it by worshipping our gods, then they can be set free.

Yours

Traianus

Trajan

Being a Christian in the Roman Empire was not easy. Christians were tortured and killed for their beliefs. They were forced to worship and bury their dead in secret. They were blamed for anything and everything that went wrong.

Source F

Whenever something bad happens – if there is an earthquake, a famine, a drought or a plague or if there is some sort of man-made disaster – the cry at once arises, 'The Christians to the lions'.

Tertullian, c. AD 200

Source G

Early Christians did not meet in churches. They met in their own houses and buried their dead in special places hidden under the ground called catacombs. This picture shows one of the catacombs in Rome.

Source E

The reason why Christians are public enemies is because they refuse to worship Emperors. They are ordinary people who worship the one true God who is more powerful than any ruler on earth.

Tertullian, c. AD 200

These Christians are the dregs of society. They are outcasts who refuse to act like normal people. No wonder it is the poorest men and women who join them. They meet secretly at night and perform strange ceremonies. They look down on our gods and our way of life.

Minucius Felix, c. AD 230

Activities

1. You are a Christian living in Rome in AD 150. Write a piece which explains:

   a) how your beliefs differ from people who are not Christians;

   b) how you are treated by people who are not Christians.

2. a) Describe the test used by Pliny. Why did he use this particular test?

   b) Why do you think Trajan told Pliny not to go looking for Christians?

3. Sources D and F show that Christians were used as a scapegoat.

   a) What is a scapegoat?

   b) Can you think of any group of people today that are used as scapegoats?

4. Why did early Christians meet in their houses and bury their dead in catacombs (Source G)?

5. Study Source E. One author was a Christian and one was not. Which was which? Explain how you know.

Decline of the Empire

Although Christians were treated badly by some Romans, the number of Christians continued to grow. One reason for this was that there was no longer peace in the Roman Empire. There was a crisis. In times of crisis, people often look for new ways of getting help. Some people believed that the Roman gods had failed to protect them and so they looked to Christianity for help.

The crisis began in the third century AD. Many Emperors were murdered and generals who wanted to become Emperor fought civil wars.

In addition, barbarian tribes from outside the Empire began to invade. Their aim was to steal money and goods that were stored in the Empire. Sometimes Emperors paid them money to return home. But this did not solve the problem because they were quick to return when they had spent it.

Taxes were increased to pay for the huge army which was needed to fight the barbarians. Prices went up and the value of money went down. Life became more difficult and less safe for everyone.

Source A

When the Emperor Pertinax had been murdered, what happened was disgraceful. Two of the candidates who wanted to be the next Emperor went to the army camp. They offered money, hoping that the soldiers would choose one of them. When one of the candidates, Julianus, made an offer of 25 000 sesterces per soldier, he was chosen as Emperor.

Dio Cassius, c. AD 210

Source B

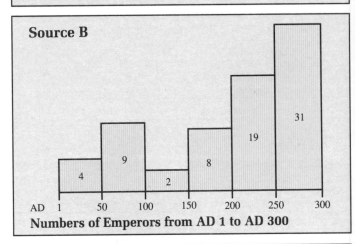

Numbers of Emperors from AD 1 to AD 300

Source C

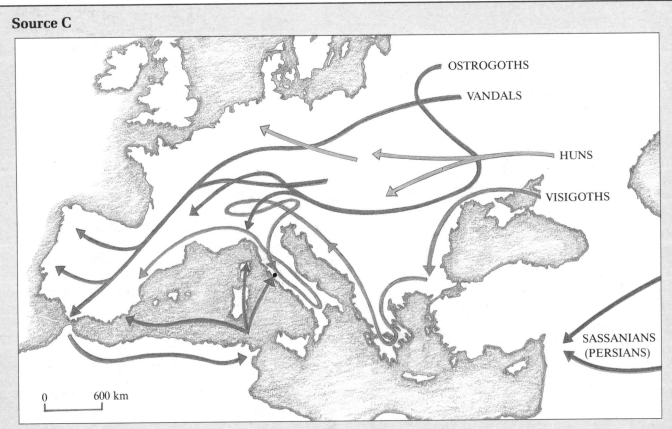

This map shows the barbarian invasions from the third century onwards.

The barbarian invasions and civil wars affected the life of people all round the Roman Empire. Attacks might happen at any time and people were forced to live in walled cities. In AD 293, the Emperor Diocletian divided the Empire into two halves, the Eastern and the Western. Although the Eastern Empire survived until 1453, the Western Empire was lost to the barbarians in AD 476.

Source D

Aquileia was the centre of Italy's wine trade. In AD 238, its population suddenly grew because crowds of refugees came there from the civil war to find safety behind the city walls.

Herodian, c. AD 245

Source E

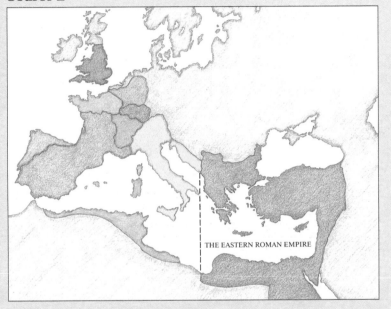

THE EASTERN ROMAN EMPIRE

By AD 476 the whole of the Western Empire had been lost. It was replaced by separate kingdoms.

Source F

In AD 260, the town of Antioch in Syria seemed peaceful. Most of the townspeople were at the theatre watching a play. It was a brilliant performance and the audience sat in silence, spellbound.

Suddenly, one of the actors shouted, 'Either I'm dreaming or the Persians are here'. The audience panicked. Weapons began to rain down on them and within minutes the town had been captured and set on fire. It soon lay in ruins with most of its people dead or wounded.

Ammianus Marcellinus, c. AD 370

Activities

1. 'From AD 200, the Roman Empire was in decline.' Explain using the sources on these pages.

2. Using Source C, make a list of barbarian tribes that invaded the Empire. Why do you think they invaded?

3. Using Sources D–F explain how the crisis affected life in the Roman Empire.

Did you know?

- The word 'barbarian' comes from the Greek. When Greek people heard foreigners talking in languages they did not understand, they thought that they sounded like sheep baaing, so they called them bar-bar-oi.

- The Romans used the word barbarian to describe anyone who lived outside the Empire. Barbarian tribes often caused great destruction. The name of one tribe was the Vandals – a word which is used today.

The rise of Christianity

The last two pages looked at the decline of the Roman Empire. At first the Christians were blamed for this decline. But, by AD 400, Christianity had become Rome's official religion. How did this happen?

AD 312 is an important date in the rise of Christianity. There was a struggle between two men to become Emperor. One of them, Constantine, ordered his soldiers to paint a Christian sign on their shields. That day, Constantine won an important victory. He went on to win more battles and by AD 324 had won control of the whole Empire.

From the time of his victory in AD 312, Constantine became a supporter of Christianity. He stopped people putting Christians to death and gave large sums of money for churches to be built. From the time of Constantine, Christianity no longer had to be a secretive religion. It became the official religion of the Roman Empire.

Source A

On the 27th October AD 312 Constantine's army camped just outside Rome. Constantine was worried. He needed something extra to help his side win. That night he had a dream. He saw a sign and a voice said, 'With this sign you will win'. The sign was two Greek letters Chi and Rho – the first two letters of Christ's name. The next morning Constantine decided to put his trust in the Christian god. Later that day, he won the battle.

Adapted from Ian Wilson, 'Jesus the Evidence', 1984

Did you know?

- The sign Constantine saw was this:

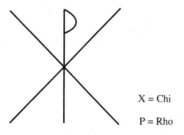

X = Chi

P = Rho

- Although he became a Christian, Constantine continued to worship other gods too. For example, on some coins he is pictured next to a sun god.

- Constantine did not always behave like a Christian. For example, in AD 326 he killed his wife by having her boiled alive in a bath and then killed his son too.

Source B

This fourth century mosaic was found in a villa in Dorset, Britain. The head is similar to those used for the old Roman gods but it is definitely the head of Jesus. This is the only Christian mosaic that has been found in Britain.

Source C

Constantine at the Council of Nicaea in AD 325. This Council made decisions about the organisation of the church that were not changed for more than 1000 years.

Source D

St Peter's church in Rome. Ever since the reign of Constantine, Rome has been a centre of Christianity. Constantine built the first church on this site.

Activities

1. Read Source A and the Did you know? box.

   Was Constantine really 'converted' to Christianity? Why did he continue to support Christianity after AD 312?

2. a) How do we know that Source B is a picture of Jesus?

   b) What does it tell us about the spread of Christianity after AD 312?

3. 'Constantine's decision in AD 312 altered the course of history.' Explain using the sources on these pages.

Checklist

- At first Christians were put to death by the Romans. The main reason for this was that they refused to worship Roman gods and to swear to obey the Emperor.

- From the third century AD the Roman Empire was in decline. There were many civil wars, and barbarian tribes invaded.

- The numbers of Christians had been growing throughout the third century. But it was only after the Emperor Constantine became a Christian that the persecution stopped and Christianity was finally accepted.

- After AD 312, Christianity became the official religion of the Roman Empire.

The Cloaca Maxima – Rome's main sewer

Public baths at Bath, Britain

Roman teacher and pupils

Themes

In AD 410 the Roman government cut off official ties with Britain. Rome had been attacked and left in ruins by the Goths. The Roman army could no longer protect a province so far away from Italy.

The collapse of the Empire did not mean the end of Rome's influence. Over the centuries Roman ideas, literature, art and architecture have affected the lives of millions of people. Rome's influence continues in the modern world.

This chapter looks at the following questions.

- What part did Roman writers play in the development of modern literature?

- How much does modern art and architecture owe to the Romans?

- How did the Roman occupation of Britain affect the development of our language?

We begin with a discussion between a group of rebels who want to overthrow Roman rule. They ask, 'What have the Romans ever done for us?'

Focus Activities

The Focus is adapted from a film entitled *The Life of Brian*, a comedy set in Roman times. It raises some interesting questions. How did the Romans change life in the provinces? Were these changes for the good?

1. The Focus page describes some of the changes that the Romans made to life in the provinces. Which change do you think was the most important? Give reasons for your answer.

2. Can you think of any other changes which have not been mentioned in the Focus?

3. Why was Chairman Reg angry?

So what have the Romans ever done for us?

It is Saturday afternoon, AD 33, and the revolutionary group, the People's Front of Judaea, are discussing the evils of life under Roman rule.

Chairman Reg   Comrades, the time has come for action. We are sick to death of these Romans. They have taken everything we've ever had – and not just from us, but from our fathers too, and from our fathers' fathers ...

Stan   And from our fathers' fathers' fathers ...

Reg   Yes, thank you, Stan ... So, they've taken everything we've got and what have they ever given us in return?

There is silence. Everybody seems to agree that the Romans haven't done anything for them when suddenly a voice from the back says...

Chairman Reg and the rebels

Voice 1   The aqueduct.

Reg   What?

Voice 1   The Romans gave us the aqueduct. Before that we never had clean drinking water.

Reg   Er, well yes, they did give us the aqueduct, that's true. But apart from the aqueduct ...?

Voice 2   Sanitation.

Stan   Oh yes, sanitation, Reg. Remember what the city used to be like? It was horrible. We didn't have sewers and the streets were full of filth.

Reg   All right, I'll grant you that the aqueduct and sanitation are two things that the Romans have done for us ...

Voice 3   And the roads. Remember the mud tracks!

Reg   (*Getting angry*) Yes, well of course the Romans built the roads, that goes without saying. But apart from the aqueduct, sanitation and the roads ...

Voices 4 & 5   Irrigation to water the crops, education, the public baths and don't forget the wine.

Stan   Yes, the wine. That's something we'd really miss if the Romans left.

Voice 6   And it's safe to walk the streets at night now, Reg.

Stan   Yes, the Romans certainly know how to keep order. And let's face it, they're the only ones who could in a town like this.

Reg   (*Very angry*) All right! But apart from the aqueduct, sanitation, irrigation, roads, education, the public baths, wine and public order, what have the Romans ever done for us?

Literature

The word 'classical' is often used to describe the literature, art and architecture of ancient Greece and Rome. 'Classical' also means 'first class' or 'of the highest standard'. The meanings are linked. Over the centuries people have judged the literature, art and architecture of ancient Greece and Rome to be 'of the highest standard'.

Roman authors followed in the footsteps of the Greeks who went before them. Roman poems, plays and histories often use and build upon what had been written by the Greeks.

Although many people in the Roman Empire could read and write, most of the literature that survives was written by or for the rich. This is most obvious if you read the work of Roman historians. They write pages and pages about the Senate and Rome's leaders, but they write very little about 'the average Roman in the street'. One reason for this is that the rich had time to write. Another reason is that writers were often supported by the rich. For example, the poets Horace and Virgil were looked after by a rich 'patron' called Maecenas (Source B). Maecenas was a friend of the Emperor Augustus.

Maecenas was a 'patron'. This means he gave money to writers and artists. They could then spend their time writing or painting.

Source A

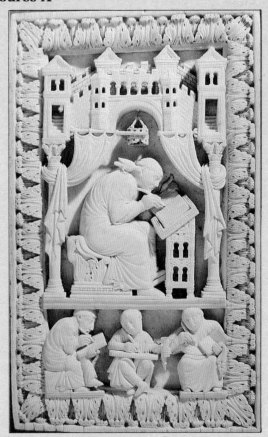

This carving shows monks making copies of books. One would read out loud while the others wrote down what he said. In this way several copies were made.

Did you know?

- The Romans wrote on scrolls made of parchment or papyrus. Paper was invented in China in c.150 BC but was unknown in Europe until AD 786.

- Printing was not invented until the 1430s. Before then, books were copied by hand.

- Some classical writing did not survive the fall of the Roman Empire. It was not until the Renaissance in the fifteenth century that much classical writing was rediscovered. Renaissance means 're-birth'.

Many writers have used their knowledge of the classical world in their writing. Shakespeare wrote plays on Roman themes – for example *Julius Caesar* and *Antony and Cleopatra*. The novelist Robert Graves wrote *I Claudius*, a novel about the Julio-Claudian Emperors. Milton's *Paradise Lost*, Dante's *Inferno* and James Joyce's *Ulysses* are all based on the classical poems written by Homer and Virgil. Knowledge of the Roman world can help us to understand what these and other authors wrote.

Source C   The Trojan War

A seventeenth century painting showing Aeneas

This is a summary of a myth told by the Greek poet Homer and the Roman poet Virgil.

- When Paris, a prince from Troy, steals a Greek woman called Helen and takes her to Troy, the Greeks sail there with an army to rescue her.

- After ten years of war, the Greeks trick the Trojans. They pretend to sail away leaving only a wooden horse. The Trojans wheel the horse into Troy, not knowing it is full of Greek soldiers.

- At night, the Greeks let themselves out of the horse and capture Troy. The Greeks then sail home.

- On the return journey, the Greek hero Odysseus is caught in a storm and separated from the others. He spends the next ten years trying to get home and has many adventures.

- The Trojan prince Aeneas leaves Troy with some friends. He spends the next ten years searching for a new home. He also has many adventures.

Activities

1. Maecenas asks you to write a short poem about his friend the Emperor Augustus. Would you praise Augustus or not? (see Chapter 4) Explain why and write the poem.

2. Look at Source A. What are the problems with making books in this way?

3. Much Roman writing has been lost. How might this affect the way in which we see the Roman Empire?

4. Source C is a summary of two famous poems. Now become a famous author.

   a) Form groups of five.
   b) Each choose one of the five episodes in Source C.
   c) Write a short story and draw pictures to go with it.
   d) Join your stories together and make a booklet.

Architecture

Many of the pictures in this book provide examples of Roman architecture. The fact that many Roman buildings still stand proves that they were well built.

Source A shows the Pantheon in Rome. This is one of the best preserved Roman buildings. It was built in c.AD 125 on the orders of the Emperor Hadrian. One reason why it is so well preserved is that it later became a church and was therefore well looked after.

Roman architecture had many links with Greek architecture. For example both use pillars and arches. This classical style was admired and copied by architects from the Renaissance onwards.

Activities

1. Make a list of the similarities between the Pantheon (Source A) and the Walker Art Gallery (Source C).

2. Are there any buildings in your area that are built in the classical style? Make a list and draw one.

3. Why do you think that Palladio (Source B) decided to build a house in this style?

4. More recent buildings in the classical style are often art galleries (Source C), museums and town halls. Why do you think this is?

5. What building materials do we have today which the Romans did not have? How has this affected the style of modern buildings?

Source A   The Pantheon, Rome

Source B   Villa Rotonda, Italy

This building was designed during the Renaissance by the Italian architect Palladio and built in 1550. Palladio used a handbook on architecture written by Vitruvius in the first century AD.

Source C   Walker Art Gallery, Liverpool

This building was designed by a Victorian architect and built in 1877.

Art

Artists from the time of the Renaissance to the present day have learned a lot from Roman art. At certain times classical art has been very popular. Often this popularity tells us something about those in power. For example, Source A shows the French leader Napoleon as a Roman Emperor about to become a god.

Roman history has also provided ideas for artists. Source B is a picture painted by Mantegna around 1480. It shows Julius Caesar's triumphant return to Rome in 46 BC. Although the theme is classical, some of the details are not. Look at the hairstyle of the man in the bottom right-hand corner.

1. a) Describe what is happening in Source A.

    b) Explain how you know that this is a classical design.

    c) Why do you think that Napoleon III – Napoleon's nephew – wanted this picture of his uncle to be painted?

2. a) What is happening in Source B?

    b) Make a list of all the things which show that this painting has a classical theme.

    c) Do you think that it is historically accurate? Give reasons for your answer.

Source A

A painting by Ingres from the reign of Napoleon III (1852-70)

Source B

A painting by Mantegna (1413-1506). He was a keen archaeologist who lived and worked in the town of Padua, North Italy.

Language

The easiest way to see how the Romans have influenced life in Britain today is to look at our language. English is a mixture of languages and includes words used by Celts, Anglo-Saxons, Vikings and the Normans. It also contains many Latin (Roman) words. Some of these words are exactly the same as those found in Latin. Others have changed slightly.

All the modern countries that once formed part of the Roman Empire still speak languages which contain a Latin element. Language is yet another way in which the Romans have made a lasting impression on history.

Did you know?

- Most educated Romans spoke Greek as well as Latin. However, Latin was always used for official purposes.

- After the collapse of the Roman Empire, people continued to write in Latin throughout the Middle Ages and beyond.

- Latin remained the official language of the Roman Catholic Church until the middle of the twentieth century.

- Many Latin phrases are still in use today. For example:
  status quo means 'the way things are',
  in camera means 'in secret'.

Source A

This picture shows the contents of a shopping basket. All the products here have one thing in common - their brand name comes from a Latin word.

Activities

1. Below is a list of Latin words. All these words are found in the English language in a slightly different form.

ambitio	mentis
auctoritas	natura
barbarus	persona
captivus	populus
industria	separo
religio	violentia

   Look at each word and think of an English word that is similar. You may be able to find several English words that come from one Latin word.

2. Look at Source A and work out why each item has been given its brand name from the list of words below.

LATIN	ENGLISH	LATIN	ENGLISH
aer	air	flora	flower
bos (bovis)	bull/ox	gala	milk
cella	cell	glacies	ice
corona	crown	lux	light
dens (dentis)	tooth	nivea	snow white
domesticus	household	saxa	rock
dura	hard	vortex	whirlpool

Source B   Coins - Roman and modern

Vitellius AD 69

George III 1819

Britannia AD 143

Britannia 1991

Activities

1. What does Source B tell us about Roman influence on the modern world?

2. Do you think that George III really looked like this (Source B)? Explain your answer.

3. a) Why do you think that January is named after the god Janus?

   b) If Septem-ber means the seventh month, what do Octo-ber, Novem-ber and Decem-ber mean?

4. What's your car called?

```
Z C B M A Q W E R T P O I I V Y A S A Y
M N O U L D L M I N I P B F E T Y A D T
A D S F F M L P O K N C I U J V I H G M
S N O V A P C O I V Y T G N J K L O P A R
A C D E R S W E D V O L V O C E D R T R
R F T G O S E D C F R T Y U I F R T Y I
W S E R M R F E D S W A Q W E R M A S N
W A C D E E Z C X M B S A W A W E Y I A O
B V C C O R T I N A M N O J V V R P L O F
A S D E R F T Y R X O K L J N H C P L F
X Z C F R Y O P F I A T K J H T E F E O
W A S B G T Y U I O P E R Y T F D X C F
A Q C A P R I C D E F T R G H V E D F R
A S D E W R T G Y D E W S A S X S F E W
D E F R T Y U H T R I U M P H A X A X F
```

Find the names of twelve makes or models of cars in the word search. All twelve names mean something in Latin.

Source C   The calendar

Our calendar is based on the one first worked out by Julius Caesar. But the Romans only had ten months in their year. The names of most of our months are Roman. For example:

JANUARY is named after the god Janus who had two faces, one looking back and one looking forward.

MARCH is named after Mars, god of war and agriculture.

JUNE is named after Juno, goddess of marriage.

JULY is named after Julius Caesar.

AUGUST is named after Augustus.

SEPTEMBER comes from 'septem' meaning 'seven' in Latin. It was the seventh month in the Roman calendar.

Checklist

- Roman and Greek art, architecture and literature are closely linked. The word classical is used to describe them.

- The Romans have influenced the modern world in many ways. From the Renaissance to the present day, the Roman world has given writers, artists and architects many ideas.

- English contains many Latin words and some Latin phrases. Many brand names are taken from Latin words.

Acknowledgements

Cover   Caroline Waring-Collins (Art Direction)

Illustrations   Susan Allen and Caroline Waring-Collins

Computer generated artwork   Elaine Marie Cox (Picatype)

Page design   Andrew Allen

Typing   Ingrid Hamer

Photography   Andrew Allen

Coins   David M. Regan, Numismatist, Southport, for advice and loan of coins

Readers   Kate Haralambos and Jane Allen, Year 7 pupils

Picture credits

Andrew Allen pp. 6 (m), 40 (b), 94, 95 (tr, br); Ancient Art and Architecture Collection pp. 12 (b), 14, 16 (l), 17, 28 (bl, br), 36, 39, 42 (b), 47, 51 (b), 53 (br), 55 (tl), 56 (t), 60 (t), 72 (t, m), 76 (bl), 78 (t), 79, 81, 88 (b), 92 (t, m); Ashmolean Museum, Oxford pp. 13, 95 (tl, bl); British Film Institute pp. 10, 89; Colchester Museums p. 42 (ml); Corinium Museum, Cirencester p. 71 (r); C.M. Dixon pp. 4 (l), 7 (t, b), 8 (b), 20, 21, 22, (t), 26, 29 (t), 32 (t), 46 (b), 53 (tl, tr, bl), 55 (b), 56 (bl, br), 58 (t), 63 (l, r), 64, 70 (m, b), 71 (l), 72 (b), 73, 75, 80, 87 (r), 88 (t, m) and cover; Mary Evans Picture Library pp. 5 (b), 49, 90; Michael Holford p. 12 (t); Mansell Collection pp. 11, 83; McDonald's Hamburgers Ltd p. 40 (t); Museum of Antiquities of the University and Society of Antiquaries of Newcastle-upon-Tyne p. 44; National Museum of Wales p. 77 (t); Nicholas On p. 76 (br); Royal Collection, reproduced by gracious permission of Her Majesty the Queen p. 93 (b); Times Books Ltd pp. 48, 54 (t); Trustees of the British Museum pp. 51 (t), 76 (t), 86; Walker Art Gallery, Liverpool p. 92 (b).

Every effort has been made to locate the copyright owners of material used in this book. Any omissions brought to our attention are regretted and will be credited in subsequent printings.

Causeway Press Ltd
PO Box 13, Ormskirk, Lancashire L39 5HP

© Steve Lancaster 1991

1st impression 1991

British Library Cataloguing in Publication Data
Lancaster, Steve
  The Roman Empire.
  I. Title
  937.06

  ISBN 0 946183 72 4

Typesetting by John A. Collins (Picatype), Ormskirk, Lancashire L39 1QR (0695) 571197
Printed and bound by Butler & Tanner Ltd, Frome and London